The Peoples of Anatolia

Ancient History

Editor-in-Chief

Lee L. Brice (*Western Illinois University*)

Editorial Board

Jeremy Armstrong (Early Rome) (*Auckland University*)
Denise Demetriou (Greece and Ancient Mediterranean)
(*University of California*)
Daniëlle Slootjes (Late Rome) (*University of Amsterdam*)
Georgia Tsouvala (Hellenistic and Roman Greece) (*Illinois State University*)

Volumes published in this Brill Research Perspectives title are listed at *brill.com/rpah*

The Peoples of Anatolia

By

Jeremy LaBuff

BRILL

LEIDEN | BOSTON

This paperback book edition is simultaneously published as issue 3.3 (2020) of *Ancient History*, DOI:10.1163/25425374-12340009

Library Congress Control Number: 2021913665

Typeface for the Latin, Greek, and Cyrillic scripts: "Brill". See and download: brill.com/brill-typeface.

ISBN 978-90-04-51950-3 (paperback)
ISBN 978-90-04-51951-0 (e-book)

Copyright 2022 by Jeremy LaBuff. Published by Koninklijke Brill NV, Leiden, The Netherlands.
Koninklijke Brill NV incorporates the imprints Brill, Brill Nijhoff, Brill Hotei, Brill Schöningh, Brill Fink, Brill mentis, Vandenhoeck & Ruprecht, Böhlau and V&R unipress.
Koninklijke Brill NV reserves the right to protect this publication against unauthorized use. Requests for re-use and/or translations must be addressed to Koninklijke Brill NV via brill.com or copyright.com.

This book is printed on acid-free paper and produced in a sustainable manner.

Contents

The Peoples of Anatolia 1
    Jeremy LaBuff
  Abstract 1
  Keywords 1
1 Introduction 1
2 Defining the Peoples of Anatolia 6
    2.1 *Lydians* 12
    2.2 *Mysians* 21
    2.3 *Karians* 24
    2.4 *Lykians* 31
    2.5 *Bithynians* 37
    2.6 *Galatians* 40
    2.7 *Phrygians?* 40
    2.8 *Other Uncertain Peoples* 45
    2.9 *Anatolians?* 52
    2.10 *Summary* 54
3 Origins 56
4 Hellenization and Other Forms of Acculturation 67
    4.1 *Language* 69
    4.2 *Culture* 73
    4.3 *Migration and Colonization* 84
5 Conclusion 89
  Acknowledgments 92
  Bibliography 92
  Index of Ancient Sources 120
  General Index 122

The Peoples of Anatolia

Jeremy LaBuff
Northern Arizona University, Flagstaff, Arizona, USA
jeremy.labuff@nau.edu

Abstract

Studies of the peoples of Anatolia take for granted the existence and importance of regional ethnic communities on the peninsula when investigating issues of identity, ethnic origins, and cultural assimilation (especially Hellenization). In reviewing the scholarship, this work argues that such assumptions lead to problematic conclusions that ignore or poorly apply recent theoretical work on ethnicity and current critiques of the assimilation model. A critical consideration of this work leads to an appreciation for the somewhat limited, and at times non-existent, role of regional ethnicity in the experiences of the inhabitants and communities of Anatolia, who mainly promoted more local forms of belonging in the face of the attempted orderings of ethnographic and imperial discourses.

Keywords

Anatolia – Asia Minor – ethnicity – Hellenization

1 Introduction

This reflective study has the awkward, if admittedly self-appointed, task of treating a topic that is comprehensively addressed by modern scholarship only rarely. There are not many (if any) 'key debates' that encompass the peoples of Anatolia as a single, discrete unit of study, unless one counts generalizations about the Hittite world or an Anatolian cultural substratum. In the first case, social history becomes an extension of empire; in the second, the connection between cultural similarity and ethnic communities remains vague. Given this historiographical situation, I should justify the topic itself before laying out the major themes for discussion.

Although its peoples are not often examined together as a whole, Anatolia itself has and continues to receive significant scholarly attention across the globe. Studies of the peninsula, or regions within it, abound, as do investigations of specific peoples, in particular those who inhabited the westernmost regions. That the most studied regions neighbor the Greek communities of the coast, the Aegean islands, and the Balkan peninsula is, of course, no mere coincidence from a discipline, ancient history, that still lingers in the shadow of Helleno-centrism (and Western-centrism). If we have more evidence from these regions, this is at least in part due to the selectivity bias of archaeological and survey work over the past two centuries. In the face of this imbalance of both evidence and scholarly treatments, an overview of the peoples of Anatolia can bring together various strands of specialization to reveal regional similarities and differences and draw attention to the entire peninsula in a way that de-centers the western end.

By 'peoples,' the relevant scholarship envisions regionally delimited ethnic communities, and I shall adopt (and test) this usage in what follows. Crucial to my understanding of what constitutes an ethnic community is the detectable presence of ethnic identity, or ethnicity, in the region in question. I elaborate on this understanding at the start of the next section, but here I want to stress that I am less interested in discussing non-ethnic forms of regional identity, a subject of recent interest among ancient historians. This is largely because the phenomenon of regionalism, as currently conceived, seems to me to conflate identification (by modern scholars) with identity (as perceived by ancient members of an ethnic region). There may be good reasons for doing so, particularly given the focus of many regional studies on 'international' economic, social or political networks.[1] Yet it is highly misleading to refer to inhabitants of regions that can be identified by modern scholars via non-ethnic parameters as 'peoples', as is the privileging of present ways of viewing the past to define who a 'people' was. It is true that there were cases of non-ethnic regional identity in the ancient Mediterranean, but few if any examples come from Anatolia.[2]

The term 'Anatolian' itself entirely follows the mandates of sensibility rather than accuracy. When I call a people or place 'Anatolian' I simply wish to locate them/it geographically. Our evidence never presumes to identify an "Anatolian" people or culture (by this or any parallel term – modern scholarship is a different story, to which we shall return). My focus in what follows is

---
1 Reger 2011; Constantakopoulou 2017, esp. 9–21; Ellis-Evans 2019, esp. 7–8.
2 See Vlassopoulos 2011, 19–22 for a fuller discussion. His list of examples include "Pontics," who largely came from communities situated on the non-Anatolian shores of the Black Sea, and Ionians, a clearly ethnic community.

on the communities of Anatolia, or Asia Minor, and specifically on its ethnic communities ('peoples'). There were thousands of Anatolian communities in antiquity, from small villages to large cities, but it is the larger groupings of these smaller communities that dominate discussions of who inhabited the peninsula and its regions.

In treating these larger entities, I omit, in part for the sake of manageability, discussion of several groups that can quite reasonably be counted as Anatolian. The Isaurians, for example, developed as a community and identity only during Late Antiquity, in complicated and not altogether connected ways to earlier groups in south-central Anatolia.[3] I also leave out the Romans, whose settlement and colonization of the region comes late enough to justify omission in the current work, except insofar as their histories intersect with that of the other peoples of Anatolia. The Armenians too receive no treatment in these pages, not only due to limited space but also because of the linguistic limitations preventing me from accessing much relevant scholarship. Related to this is the fact that Armenia, although equally situated in Anatolia and the Caucasus, tends to be studied by scholars focusing on the latter region. A change to this situation is desirable, but must take its inspiration from one who specializes in Armenian studies.[4]

Finally, I lend but peripheral attention to the Greek coastal communities. Like that of the Armenians, the topics of Greek, Ionian, Aiolian, and Dorian identities deserve fuller discussion than I can present here, but these topics are also complicated by key differences in relation to other Anatolians. Most obviously, they refer to identities that were not defined exclusively (or even mainly) within and in reference to Anatolian territory. The question of what it meant to be Greek in Anatolia cannot be answered without leaving Anatolia entirely. This is less true for the Ionian, Dorian, and (possibly) Aiolian communities on the peninsula, who developed a sense of ethnic commonality through shared sanctuaries and festivals; nevertheless, they came to understand their regional ethnicity in relation to non-Anatolian homelands and identities.[5] The contrast with other Anatolian groups is significant: as we will see, Bithynians were thought by Greeks (and possibly Persians) to be Thracian migrants, but they neither celebrated such origins nor self-identified as Thracian themselves. We can largely limit our gaze to Bithynia to understand Bithynian identity and its importance to members of this ethnic community, something that is not true for Ionians or Dorians. The point here is not to deny that these groups were

---

3 Burgess 1990; Syme 1995, 217–19.
4 See, e.g., Burney and Lang 1971; Hovannisian 1997.
5 Ionians: Mac Sweeney 2021; Aiolians: Rose 2008; Dorians: J. Hall 2002, 82–89.

Anatolian – they were – but to highlight the greater entanglement of their identities with other communities outside Anatolia that makes a proper treatment here too difficult. At the same time, the deeply intertwined histories of Greek and non-Greek communities in Anatolia means that we cannot neglect the former entirely, especially when it comes to the impact of outside political and cultural influences, discussed below.

The chronological focus is the first millennium BCE, when the peoples of Anatolia are thought to have existed in their most coherent form. Yet attention will also be paid to what scholars have concluded about the Bronze Age – the focus of discussions on ethnic origins – and the Roman Imperial period, where questions of ethnic survival and 'acculturation' attract scholarly attention. I am less interested in a history of events than in understanding what it meant to belong to one (or more) of these ethnic groups, and how this sense of belonging evolved over time.

Studies that treat this topic for particular regions typically seek to answer one or more of three major questions. First, who were the peoples of Anatolia? The answer to this question is usually sought from ethnographic writers like Herodotos and Strabo, whose lists and descriptions provide the categories to which other evidence is fitted, including inscriptions in local languages, material culture assemblages, and Greek epigraphical attestations of ethnic terms or linguistically Anatolian names. Taken together, this evidence is challenging to interpret because often ambiguous in significance, and typically sparse for each people in question, as we will see. Second, scholars seek to understand the origins of Anatolian peoples, usually with respect to migration from elsewhere or Bronze Age antecedent indigenous groups. Crucial to this work is the linguistic analysis of Anatolian languages and Hittite ethnographic terms. Finally, studies investigate the impact of outside influence on Anatolian peoples, usually through concepts like Hellenization and other forms of acculturation, to track the disappearance of markers of regional ethnic identity, especially during the Hellenistic and Roman periods. Here, processes of language and cultural change as attested in the epigraphical and archaeological records are central.

In tackling these three questions, this work aims, in addition to bringing more specialized studies into conversation with each other, to challenge the assumptions that underlie many of the scholarly approaches and answers to these issues. I argue that the question of "who?" must be preceded by a question of "did x people exist?" and followed by a question of how important identifying with a given people was to the supposed members of that ethnic community. The first section thus surveys the major ethnic groups discussed by scholars, focusing on the first millennium BCE, with an eye to moving beyond the basic issue of identification, and examining what defined these ethnic groups, and to what extent ethnic belonging mattered to its purported members. While the reality and importance of ethnicity is generally taken for granted by most scholars, I will show that regional ethnic identity often mattered very little to many Anatolians, to the point of having an undetectable impact on their behaviors and expressions in the evidence that survives.

The next section dispenses with the assumption of the existence, across time, of the peoples named in our Greek and Roman sources, and explores what this move entails for the question of ethnic origins. Abandoning this assumption pushes us to move away from current discussions of origins that simply equate language or Hittite ethnographic terms with later ethnic groups of Anatolia, and to approach the question through the framework of ethnogenesis. Current scholarly assumptions, I argue, are methodologically unsound and cause us to overlook the constructed nature of ethnicity and, therefore, to become inattentive to historically contingent processes of ethnogenesis. Rather than simply taking for granted that such groups existed in relatively stable form across centuries, I ask how later groups came to perceive themselves as ethnic communities and how such origins should inform our understanding of who they were.

In a final section, I turn to the fraught issue of Hellenization and other forms of 'acculturation,' which constitutes the dominant, but not unchallenged, model for understanding cultural change on the peninsula between the mid-first millennium BCE and the early centuries of the common era. In treating the impact of Greek cultural influence on and eventual political domination over the peoples of Anatolia, the typical scholarly study paints a narrative either of one-way assimilation of Anatolians to Greek culture and identity, or of a more reciprocal set of interactions that still results in Anatolians becoming Greek, but in which Greekness itself incorporates or accommodates Anatolian elements. Making use of the critiques of the concept of Hellenization both inside and outside the field of Anatolian studies, I will argue for an abandonment of this concept in favor of an understanding of cultural interaction and change less dependent on an identitarian methodology. Such a methodology not only takes for granted the importance of regional ethnic identities, including 'Greekness,' but inexplicably insists on understanding Greek culture and identity as oppositional to, or at least fundamentally distinct in origin from, the regional and local cultures and identities within Anatolia. This insistence ignores the deeply intertwined histories of Anatolia and the 'Greek world' that predate the very existence of Greekness and reveal the acculturation model as inadequate.

2   Defining the Peoples of Anatolia

Who were the peoples of Anatolia? While many scholars take for granted that these communities were regionally delimited and self-evident, some studies have spent more focused attention on defining one or more of these peoples, resulting in three major (and often overlapping) approaches. The first is to follow the categories and accounts of Greco-Roman ethnography, particularly those of 'global' ethnographers like Herodotos and Strabo. The second is to equate ethnic communities with the traces of their languages, both as distinct tongues and as names with non-Greek origin, that appear in written (especially epigraphic) texts. Finally, attempts are made to associate particular forms of material culture with one or more Anatolian ethnic groups. In this section, I will discuss each major ethnic community in relation to these three approaches, in order to establish which purported groups imagined themselves to be ethnic communities, in what ways, and to what extent.

Before proceeding, it is worth briefly considering these approaches in relation to the theories of ethnicity currently dominant in the field of ancient history. Most influential in this regard, and to my own understanding of the concept, is the work of Jonathan Hall, whose dissemination and modification of Anthony Smith's conceptualization of ethnicity, stresses five key aspects. To paraphrase, this ethnic identity involves (a) self-constitution in opposition to other groups; (b) membership determined, at minimum, by myths of shared kinship, attachment to homeland, and a sense of a common history ('core elements'); (c) other possible markers of identification, such as physiognomy, language, religion, or other aspects of culture ('secondary *indicia*'); (d) dynamism and fluidity, rather than possessing a static nature or fixed boundaries; and (e) not always being the most important identity.[6] Aspect (a) means privileging *emic* evidence – i.e., evidence internally produced by a community or its members, such as inscribed decrees, epitaphs, or locally produced histories and material culture – when determining the existence and nature of a given ethnicity, over *etic* perspectives (produced from a vantage point outside of the community). Aspects (b) and (c) argue for the priority of evidence that reveals the presence of core elements as opposed to secondary *indicia*. Aspects (d) and (e) remind us that evidence for ethnicity in one period cannot automatically

---

6   J. Hall 2002, 9–19; Smith 1986. I omit a sixth key feature since it refers to what "often" occurs rather than something inextricably linked with all instances of ethnic self-identification. Cf. Ruby 2006 for important modifications.

be translated forward or backward, or be taken to represent a primary way of identifying with others.[7]

Keeping in mind this understanding of what it means to be a people, let us turn to the three major approaches to defining the peoples of Anatolia. The emphasis on emic evidence is at odds with the first approach, which relies on the ethnographic writings of, especially, Greek writers. Although ethnographic lists of Anatolian peoples date back to Homer, most scholars view the epic as important for questions of origins, but not as foundational for understanding the identities of the historical peoples of Anatolia. Instead, this honor is reserved for Herodotos. His view of the ethnic makeup of the region is encapsulated in two passages: his accounts of the Persian satrapies and of Xerxes' military contingents. According to the first (3.89–90), each satrapy consisted of a collection of peoples (*ethnê*), among which the westernmost included 'Ionians, the Magnesians in Asia, Aiolians, Karians, Lykians, Milyans, and Pamphylians.' The next satrapy encompassed Lydians, Mysians, Lasonians, Kabalians, and Hytennians. A third consisted of Phrygians, Asian Thracians, Paphlagonians, Mariandynians, and Syrians, and a fourth was equivalent to the land of the Kilikians.[8] The second passage, recounting the various ethnic contingents in Xerxes' army, aligns with the first in identifying Paphlagonians, Mariandynians, Syrians, Phrygians, Lydians, Mysians, Asian Thracians, Milyans, Kilikians, Pamphylians, Lykians, Karians, Ionians, and Aiolians, but also contains some interesting additions and modifications (7.72–77, 91–95). Here we learn that these Syrians are also called Kappadokians, that the Asian Thracians are actually called Bithynians, that the Kabalians are the same as Lasonians, and hear of several new ethnic groups, including Ligyes, Matieni (both of whom seem to neighbor the Paphlagonians), and Dorians, whom he had already identified earlier in his work (1.144). The name of one group (at 7.76) that should likely be located in Anatolia has been lost from surviving manuscripts: perhaps it is the Hytennians, since the only other people mentioned (at 3.90), the Magnesians, were likely included with the Ionians.

---

7 Subsequent critiques of Hall tend to accept his theoretical premises but to question his implementation (e.g., Vlassopoulos 2015) or to prefer emic definitions of ethnicity that deny that specific criteria mark ethnic identity across historical exempla (e.g., Konstan 2001; cf. Siapkas 2014). See a response to both critiques in J. Hall 2015.

8 After cycling through Southwest Asia, Egypt, and Central Asia, Herodotos lists as the "thirteenth" satrapy the region of Pakytê and Armenia (3.93), suggesting that he sees this region as distinct from Anatolia. By contrast at 7.73 he claims that the Armenians were descendants of Phrygians and served under the same commander (a Persian noble).

MAP 1   Anatolia
SOURCE: TINA ROSS ARCHAEOLOGICAL ILLUSTRATIONS

THE PEOPLES OF ANATOLIA

This list has served as the basis, though not the exact blueprint, for ethnographic knowledge of the peninsula among subsequent Greco-Roman writers and modern scholars alike. From this list, a distinction is made between 'major' ethnic groups, about which we know significantly more from other sources, and the rest. To the former category are assigned, besides Greeks (Ionians, Aiolians, and Dorians), Karians, Lykians, Pamphylians, Lydians, Mysians, Bithynians, Paphlagonians, Kappadokians, and Kilikians. The rest are either ignored or equated with later 'major' ethnic groups, like the Pisidians, who seem to inhabit a region similar to the Milyans, Kabalians/Lasonians, and Hytennians. To be fair, a good reason for this latter decision is that most of these other ethnic groups are hardly ever (or never) mentioned again by sources.

In reality, Herodotos' lists tell us who he thought the peoples of Anatolia were, but not necessarily whether this was how things were understood by the inhabitants of the region. The source for not just Herodotos' information, but for the very categories he uses to ethnically map out Anatolia has not been as much the subject of modern inquiry as perhaps it should be. I will discuss some cases where it is likely that he consulted local sources, but more generally there is good reason to think that Herodotos was neither inventing these categories nor, in most cases, consulting Anatolians themselves, but instead adopting the worldview of the Persian Empire.[9] More than half a century before Herodotos, the Persian King Darius envisioned his empire as inhabited by peoples (*dahyava*) whom he listed on several royal inscriptions to convey the extent of his rule. The number of peoples whom he locates in Anatolia is somewhat shorter than what Herodotos provides, but the king's lists operate according to the same organizing principle: he mentions the Kappadokians (*Katpatuka*), Lydians (*Sparda*), Karians, Thracians (*Skudra*, which could include the Bithynians), and Greeks (*Yauna*).[10] He was also aware of the Lykians, whom contemporary worker lists from Persia refer to by their indigenous name, *termilai*.[11] The fact that Herodotos specifically mentions the Persians as his source for calling "Syrians" Kappadokians also strengthens the idea that his own ethnography was inspired by Achaemenid imperial categories, as does the rough equivalence between his list and Ktesias' conception of the empire's Anatolian holdings, which Llewelyn-Jones argues reflects a Persian perspective.[12]

---

[9] See, e.g., Haubold 2013, 100–17. This worldview was itself descended from Neo-Assyrian ideologies of conquest and empire.

[10] Briant 2002, 172–83, discussing the Susian foundation charters (*DSz, DSaa*) and the Achaemenid "country lists" (*DB, Dpe, DNa, Dse,* and *XPh*). Cf. Henkelman and Stolper 2009 on the Skudra as referring to the northwestern inhabitants of the empire in flexible fashion.

[11] On these lists, see Schmitt 2003; Tavernier 2015.

[12] Llewlyn-Jones and Robson 2010, 2.3 and 55–68.

Herodotos' list also does not tell us much about what made someone Karian, Lykian, etc., though in other parts of his work he is often interested in exploring this question. His famous 'definition' of Greekness suggests that shared kinship, religion, language, and customs work together to inform the sense of commonality within any ethnic group (8.144), a view that has subsequently shaped the criteria by which many modern scholars have sought to define the various ethnic communities of Anatolia.[13] They generally identify shared kinship in the literary evidence, the shared language through linguistic studies, and common religion and customs via the material record. Yet this rough alignment with Hall's theory of ethnicity is surface-level, in part since it ignores the fact that Herodotos' definition is problematic because it is not representative of the views of most Greeks or even Herodotos himself.[14] More importantly, the application of this theory in Anatolian studies tends to be selective and lacking in rigor. The tendency to use Herodotos as a beginning is a case in point, since neither the historian from Halikarnassos, who lived for a time in Athens, nor his ethnographic successors, can provide the emic point-of-view on which Hall's 'core elements' of ethnicity all depend. Linguistic evidence, the second major approach to our topic mentioned above, might be thought to constitute emic evidence, but this is to ignore the role of language in Hall's (and Smith's) definition as a secondary *indicium* of ethnic identity. The same can be said for approaches that focus on material culture. Both language and culture *can* indicate ethnic belonging, but what is needed is evidence that they actually did for the peoples in question. Rarely is such evidence looked for even when available.

Nevertheless, to appraise a field of study we must begin with its categories. In this section, I consider in turn the major ethnic groups as identified by Herodotos, plus groups like the Pisidians and Galatians who became prominent in subsequent evidence. After tracing, commenting upon, and often critiquing efforts to identify and define each people of Anatolia, I explore the emic evidence and institutional basis for these ethnic identities, a crucial factor occasionally but insufficiently discussed by modern scholarship, to argue against the view that regional ethnic identities like 'Lydian' and 'Karian' were primary or consistently present for most inhabitants of Anatolia, and to call into question the very existence of many ethnic identities attributed to these inhabitants by external commentators, whether Greek, Roman, or modern.

---

[13] Invoked, for example, by Hönigmann and Oettinger 2018, 105–07.

[14] See Gruen 2020, 42–55 on the problems with taking this passage as a definition that most Greeks, or even Herodotos himself, endorsed.

2.1 Lydians

Hönigmann and Oettinger's recent study of Lydia explains why the simplistic reliance on Herodotos of earlier studies leads to an erroneous understanding of the region's history. While he has much to tell us of the Lydian kingdom, and the Lydian people that constituted its core inhabitants, they allege that he imposes foreign (especially Greek) elements into his account of the Lydian past that must be "restored" through a combination of textual criticism (similar to historicist approaches to the Old Testament) and consideration of other evidence, most importantly Lydian texts. A key example of this process is their rejection of Herodotos' derivation of the Lydians' name from a distant king called Lydos, about whom we otherwise know very little (1.7). They argue that such eponymous ancestry represents a Greek schema inserted, along with the figure of Herakles, into a narrative that only provides Lydian names from Gyges on.[15] I would add that Herodotos' understanding is both shaped by imperial categories, since the Persian satrapy based in Sardis was no doubt itself based on the kingdom that Cyrus conquered, and in conflict with them, since he prefers the Greek term "Lydian" (Λύδοι) to Persian *Sparda* or Lydian *sfarda*.

We might, however, be going too far if we dispense with Herodotos entirely as an author who simply incorporates the "Lydians" into the Greek mythological universe, since the figure of Lydos also shows up in a Lydian source. Herodotos' rough contemporary, Xanthos of Lydia, whose work only survives in fragments, agrees that Lydos was the namesake of the people (*FGrH* 765 F16).[16] Both Xanthos and Herodotos also claim that the neighboring Mysians were originally Lydian colonists (F15; Hdt. 7.74.2). This suggests that crucial claims about the origins of the Lydian ethnonym itself derive from Lydian sources.[17] It also suggests that shared kinship featured in what it meant to be Lydian. Lydos' name implies status as an eponymous ancestor of the entire community. And yet things are also not that simple. For one, according to this account, the Lydian people predated Lydos, known beforehand as Meiones (Hdt. 1.7; cf. *Iliad* 2.864), which would mean that plenty of Lydians were not, by the logic

---

15 Hönigmann and Oettinger 2018, 17–22, 65–95. Regarding the Heraklid genealogy of the Lydian kings, they argue that this was either a Greek invention or propaganda by later Lydian rulers to foster links with Sparta. In the latter case, it is unclear how royal propaganda can be distinguished from Lydian tradition if the very idea of a Lydian people existed within the framework of the monarchical state.

16 Mehl 2003. Both ancient authors also include a fairly similar version of the Gyges myth.

17 Cf. Burkert 1995, who persuasively argues that the interlinking of dynastic genealogies originates with the Lydian Mermnads rather than Greek mythographers and historians. For an extended discussion of what can and cannot be trusted in Herodotos' treatment of the Lydians, in the context of other literary, epigraphical, and linguistic evidence, see Hönigman and Oettinger 2018, 65–119.

of the myth, descendants of Lydos but of the Meiones. Whether or not this factored in the thought process of self-described Lydians is impossible to know.

A second complication is that Herodotos and what survives from Xanthos are not concerned with defining who counted as Lydian. Despite their critical approach to Herodotos, Hönigmann and Oettinger take it as an article of faith that the Lydians were a people defined by both the institutional framework of the Lydian state and use of the Lydian language, an assumption in turn based on how Herodotos describes the Lydians and on his inclusion of language in his definition of Greekness.[18] Yet the very concept of a world made up of *ethnê* might represent a 'Greek' schema. Moreover, many of the later kings conquered Greek and other non-Lydian peoples, without these new subjects becoming Lydian, and we remain ignorant of the administrative structures of the empire. As a result, it is difficult to determine how many subjects of the Lydian kings felt a sense of shared kinship with their kings.[19] Was Herodotos merely extrapolating from these kings to fit the inhabitants of 'Lydia' within his ethnographic framework?

The issue did not gain clarity over time. Under Augustus, Strabo admits uncertainty about where to find Lydians, thanks in part to the confusion of his sources, which conflate Lydians and Phrygians, *inter alia* (14.3.3).[20] He finds Lydians in Sardis and its environs, though even here living alongside Mysians and Macedonians (13.4.6). They are not in Philadelphia or Thyateira, which he sees as Mysian and Macedonian, respectively, and he is unsure whether the Katakekaumenê district is Mysian or Meionian. To the south of this region, he finds ethnic mixing among Lydians, Mysians, Phrygians, Karians, and Ionians (13.4.12). How he makes these identifications is also unclear, since he does not reveal his sources and admits that the Lydian language is no longer spoken in the region (13.4.17).

The implication of Strabo's confusion is that we cannot assume that all inhabitants of Lydia, the region of the Lydian kingdom when shorn of its conquered territories, thought of themselves as Lydian.[21] His uncertain criteria for identifying them reveals a tension between a Greek ethnographic expectation that ethnic groups will be geographically coherent and a much more complex landscape of communal identities.[22] In his overview of the entire Anatolian peninsula, Strabo organizes the region by peoples – Paphlagonians, Phrygians,

---

18   Hönigman and Oettinger 2018, 93–107.
19   See Hönigmann and Oettinger 2018, 102–105 on the distinction between the Lydian rulers (especially the Mermnads) and the Lydian people in Herodotos.
20   Cf. Baldriga 1997.
21   For this assumption, see Roosevelt 2003, 2.
22   Salmeri 2000, esp. 167.

Lykaonians, Bithynians, Mysians, Greeks, Karians, Lykians, Lydians – or districts – Epiktetos, the Troad, Hellespontia. While the districts already do not fit into his predominantly ethno-geographical schema, when he comes to explore the peoples he lists, he acknowledges a much more complex picture, as we have seen in the case of Lydia.[23] The reason must lie in his sources, which do not seem to have been the inhabitants of the region, but largely earlier written works.[24] If these sources disagreed about where each people lived, as with the Katakekaumenê, then this would explain his solution to call such regions ethnically mixed without reference to specific communities. The probability that both Strabo and his sources represent an external ethnographic perspective holds true for earlier Greek works, including Herodotos himself, except where we can prove otherwise.[25] If we ascribe to an understanding of identity as a construct produced by the group itself, then these literary sources must be considered of secondary importance in favor of whatever emic evidence we can uncover for how the inhabitants of Lydia self-identified.

As we have seen, Hönigmann and Oettinger value Lydian language texts as the most important body of emic evidence for reconstructing Lydian history and identity. This corpus has led to significant insights that earlier scholars were unaware of, thanks to the impressive recent work in decipherment.[26] We will look in the next section at how historical linguistics makes use of this evidence to uncover the origins of the Lydians themselves.[27] Yet Lydian texts are also studied to track the habitation and movement of Lydians in later periods. The surviving corpus of Lydian inscriptions mostly comes from or near Sardis, and some of the exceptions are found in locations that we can be confident never identified as Lydian, such as Pergamon and Ephesos.[28] These likely reflect the immigration of Lydians, especially to coastal Greek cities.[29] At the same time, according to Strabo (13.4.17), Lydian was still being spoken in his own day as one of the four major languages, along with Pisidian, Solymean, and Greek, of Kibyra, a city situated far from Lydia in the area east of Karia, north of Lykia, south of Phrygia, and west of Pisidia. He links the presence of

---

23 For the primarily ethnic framework of Strabo's description of Anatolia, see Mitchell 2000, 119–22.
24 Salmeri 2000, 179–80.
25 Strabo does cite Xanthos on occasion (13.4.9, 11). For a more trusting view of Greek sources on Lydia, see Seel 1956.
26 For a recent summary of this work, see Payne and Wintjes 2016, 6, 63–82.
27 E.g., Hönigman & Oettinger 2018, 105–107.
28 Bielfeldt 2019, 167–72; Payne 2019, 232–33. For the inscriptions from Pergamon and Ephesos, see Gusmani et al., #40, #48, and #52.
29 Kerschner 2010, 261–62.

Lydian here to a Lydian colonization of the region, possibly as part of Croesus' expansion in the sixth century.

There are, however, challenges to using language to identify Lydians. Strabo does not indicate that any Kibyretans saw themselves as Lydian, and certainly no epigraphical evidence from the city suggests this. More importantly, we have no way of tracking with any accuracy the boundaries of where the language was spoken natively, and Lydian identity seems to have far outlived public expressions of the language. Written texts disappear after the fourth or early third centuries BCE in favor of the Greek language, while Strabo, as we have seen, informs us that Lydian was no longer spoken in Lydia itself by his day. Regardless of the truth of this claim, his statement surely must reflect a contemporary impression stemming from interaction with people from Lydia (whether in the region or not), who did not publicly project any competence in the language. The inevitable conclusion is that during Roman times, and probably for a considerable part of the Hellenistic period, the Lydian language was not an important component of what it meant to be Lydian. Perhaps it was beforehand, but if so we must ask why the language was abandoned not only in written but also in spoken form by those who most publicly represented Lydian identity to the wider world, or at least to intellectuals like Strabo.

There is one indication that in the Classical period, at least, language did inform Lydian identity, but with unexpected implications. A fragment from Xanthos' lost history tells us that Lydos had a brother, Torhebos, who like Lydos became the ruler of a people named after him, the Torhebians, who spoke a language similar to Lydian in the way that Dorian relates to (and differs from) Ionian (F15). While this tale morphs into an account of the Lydian colonization of Etruria in Herodotos, with "Torhebos" becoming "Tyrrhenos" (1.94), it is clear from another fragment of Xanthos that Torhebia was located in Anatolia near Lydia.[30] The implication is that what Greeks like Herodotos perceived as an ethnically coherent monolith was split in fifth-century Lydian minds, and probably earlier as well, into at least two distinct ethnic groups, Lydians and Torhebians, who were related but distinct both in identity and language.[31] The Xanthos fragment alerts us not only to the greater ethnic diversity in Lydia than is discussed by modern scholars, but also to the fact that written Lydian

---

30 Preserved in Nikolaos of Damascus (*FGrH* 90 F15). Cf. Bengisu 1994. Interestingly, Herodotos ascribes his version to Lydian sources.
31 A passage from Aischylos' *Persians* (49–52) also may refer to the Torhebians by the poetic name *Tharybis*, as well as another group associated with *Mardon*. Cf. Bengisu 1994, 40–42. Her suggestion that Mardon refers to settlements in Lydia by the Iranian Mardoi (Hdt. 1.125) is possible, but it could also be linked with the Lydian river and king, Masdnes/Masnes, on which see Robert 1937, 155–58.

may give a false impression of linguistic unity where spoken dialects contained enough differences to help define how being Lydian was distinct from being Torhebian. Language thus serves here as a marker of local variation within the region, something the script may not convey.[32]

Related to the use of language to identify Lydians is the scholarly tendency to attribute linguistically Lydian names to Lydian individuals, especially when looking at later periods of Lydian history.[33] This assumption contains the same problems just discussed with reference to the language: linguistically similar names may mask important differences among Lydians, Torhebians, and even Mysians.[34] At the same time, the long history of contact among Greeks, non-Greek Anatolians, and Persians in Lydia would have meant that onomastic borrowings would not have necessarily had any impact on the ethnic identity of those bearing Greek (or Iranian) names.

If not language, then what of religion? The challenge is in defining what we mean by a 'Lydian' religion, especially given the close relationship between 'Lydian' and 'Greek' gods.[35] If we mean the religious activity of 'Lydians,' then we have unhelpfully sidestepped the question. If we mean religious activity that expressed the communal bonds of the Lydian ethnic group, then we must look for cults that either explicitly or implicitly allude to a Lydian identity.

The candidates alluding to such an identity are few before the Roman period, but worth noting. Artemis was clearly an important deity in the region, with cults at Sardis and Koloë.[36] In Lydian, the former was called *artimus sfardav* (*LW* 11), which can be translated as Sardian or Lydian Artemis. This sanctuary lay outside the city walls as well, suggesting more regional importance, which is perhaps why it was monumentalized during the Seleukid revitalization of the city.[37] Moreover, we know that religious bonds linked communities in the region radiating out from Mount Tmolos, especially the middle Hermos and

---

32 Cf. the prominent bilingual Greek-Lydian inscription on the temple of Athena/Malis at Pergamon (*IvP* 1.1). If this is an attempt to portray the sanctuary as appealing to two distinct traditions, as suggested by Bielfeldt 2019, 172, then the tradition associated with the Lydian inscription may show how Mysians used this language as well.
33 Gauthier 1989, 160–70; Spawforth 2001, 384–86.
34 Cf. Roosevelt 2009, 85–89, though he focuses more on the accommodation of neighboring peoples, especially Greeks and Phrygians.
35 Hönigman and Oettinger 2018, 74–80.
36 Payne 2019, 233, 240. Payne's assumption that the temple represents Ephesian Artemis (see previous note) does not make sense of the ability of the cult to develop into the chief civic cult in Sardis.
37 Yegül 2019, 132–42.

Kayster river valleys.³⁸ Sacred roads connected Sardis to Hypaipa and Koloë, the site of an important sanctuary to Artemis.³⁹ The relationship between these local cults and the equally important cult of Ephesian Artemis worshiped by 'Lydians' at both Sardis and Ephesos is less clear.⁴⁰ Is the latter a foreign import and forerunner or influence on the Artemis cults at Sardis and Koloë, or should we see all three cults as originally distinct and only subsequently connected? In any case, if Lydians typically worshiped Artemis, this practice did not distinguish them from neighboring Greeks, especially if, as some scholars argue, worship of Artemis was borrowed from the Greeks. And from the third century BCE, Sardian Artemis shared a temple with Zeus Polieus, suggesting that she had by then become associated specifically with civic identity.⁴¹

More indirectly, we can try to distinguish cults in Lydia that were rooted in the local landscape from what seem like external (Greek, Persian, Egyptian) imports. One study has identified the vast majority of so-called "Lydian" cults as "Anatolian," with particular persistence of this grouping in eastern Lydia.⁴² The prominence of Kufawa/Kybebe in our surviving evidence is an example.⁴³ Yet "Anatolian" cannot definitively stand in as a synonym for "Lydian," not only because the term encompasses ethnic groups outside of Lydia (e.g., Phrygian), but because it reflects an outside, modern observation of cultural similarities, such as the widespread worship of a mother goddess, that were not clearly perceived or expressed by the various communities of Lydia. In the end, one gets the impression that such labels for religious activity matter more for modern scholars who have assumed the significance of ethnic identity and difference than it did for ancient practitioners concerned with more local forms of belonging.

What about material culture as an expression of Lydian identity? The most promising evidence consists of the many elite tumuli scattered through the region, which reveal a burial practice that was fairly uniform and an expression of shared elite regional values especially prevalent in the first century of Achaemenid rule.⁴⁴ These practices die out in the fourth century, however.

---

38   For a definition of Lydia that includes also the upper stretches of these valleys, along with their main tributaries and the Upper Kaikos valley, see Roosevelt 2019, 147–48.
39   Roosevelt 2009, 129–33.
40   Lydian inscriptions from Sardis (LW 1, 2, 24, 25, 54) invoke *artimus ipsimsis*.
41   Payne and Wintjes 2016, 97–100. Cf. de Hoz 2016, 185–221.
42   De Hoz 1999. Cf. Payne 2019.
43   Yet there is nothing to support the assertion that she was the "supreme god" of the Lydians, nor was she "equated with Artemis," as claimed by Marek 2016, 115. Cf. the more tentative discussion in Hönigman and Oettinger 2018, 115–16.
44   Roosevelt 2019, 148–50, noting also that the trailing off of these burial types reflects a reduction of the importance of this elite from the late fifth century. Cf. Baughan 2010.

Elite networks seem to resurface in the Hellenistic period, when we find non-Sardian elites performing acts of benefaction in the city, and Sardian elites doing the same in central Lydia.[45] Such actions are ambiguous with respect to ethnic motivation. Other possibilities include domestic pottery styles or local forms of dedicatory stelai, but these seem largely restricted to Sardis and its environs, making it difficult to know how widespread such forms would have been, not to mention whether such similarities would have been perceived as important.[46]

Before the Roman period, then, we do not find many clear expressions of Lydian identity from Lydia itself. To explain why, it may be helpful to recount the institutional history of the region. Before the Persian conquest, Lydian identity can be linked to the monarchy, and perhaps the regional elite. This was certainly how archaic Greek poets perceived it, who mostly referred to Lydians in connection with Croesus or the Lydian army.[47] What this meant for the rest of the population is uncertain. The Persian period brought an end to direct political institutions that might foster a common Lydian identity, especially after the failure of Paktyes' revolt, and even the memory of Croesus' kingdom "ceased to be a significant factor in the Lydian consciousness."[48] While the Persian kings certainly understood this part of their realm as "Lydian" (*Sparda*), it is unclear whether administrative structures existed which would have reinforced an earlier Lydian self-consciousness, or if the inclusion of multiple ethnic groups in the satrapy based at Sardis worked to efface Lydian identity.

At the same time, significant land in the region was colonized by Iranian elites and soldiers who were granted agricultural estates, especially from the late fifth century.[49] As usual, the details remain obscure, but these settlements surely fragmented the geographical cohesion of the Lydian ethnic community, as did the de-urbanization of Sardis, by placing many of its inhabitants under the fiscal authority of Iranian landlords.[50] The trend of fragmentation continued into the Hellenistic period, where at least eighteen settlements of Macedonian veterans were established in Lydia, though many may have

---

45   Roosevelt 2009, 132.
46   For the view that these items expressed "Lydian cultural mores," see Berlin 2019.
47   Croesus: Bacchylides 3; Military: Mimnermos 13, Sappho 16; cf. Sappho 96, referring to the addressee as conspicuous among "Lydian women," where earlier in the poem Sardis seems to be mentioned in a fragmentary line.
48   Rung 2015, 22.
49   Sekunda 1985, 7–30; Roosevelt 2003 and 2009, 197–200.
50   On the large-scale depopulation and change in location of habitation of Achaemenid Sardis, see Cahill 2019, 11–23.

replaced Iranian settlements.[51] And one wonders if the Mysians that Strabo observes as inhabiting central Lydia alongside Lydians and Macedonians (see above) were the result of Attalid military settlements in the second century. In the face of all these changes, did the prior inhabitants preserve a sense of commonality with other Lydians or develop more local identities tied to village and urban communal life?

Alongside this regional situation, Sardis evolved into a more publicly self-aware community under the Seleukids. While continuing to function as the administrative center for Seleukid imperial holdings in western Anatolia, as it had for the Achaemenids, Sardis re-urbanized and developed civic political institutions, such as a council, assembly, and elected magistracies, that would have strengthened a Sardian identity.[52] Yet it is striking that the city's tribe names evoke figures from the central Lydian landscape (Tymolis, Masdnis) or remote and royal Lydian history (Dionysias, Pelopis, Mermnas).[53] In configuring (or reconfiguring) their history as an integral part of their identity, it seems that Sardian history was Lydian history. But was Lydian history also Sardian history, i.e., was there a sense of Lydian history (and identity) beyond the confines of the Sardian community?

In the Archaic and early Classical periods, this was likely the case, given the Lydian name for Lydians: *sfardêti*.[54] The equivalence of this ethnic with the capital of the Lydian kingdom (Sardis in Greek) is no coincidence, and strongly suggests that the ethnic community was not just centered on, but defined by, the urban community. That *sfardêti* is a Lydian word makes it likely that this was an emic conception of the Lydian community that radiated out to their Persian overlords, who pronounced the term *Sparda*.[55] But the depopulation of the city under the Achaemenids seems to have at first diffused Lydian identity among the elite, if the tumuli burials can be seen as an effort to retain a connection to the Mermnad period, and then after a century led to a weakening of these associations. The subsequent resurgence of Sardis as a city and its development of autonomous civic institutions appear to have emphasized Sardian identity defined in terms of the urban space and its immediate hinterland, at least for most of the Hellenistic period. If this development also implicated Lydian identity, it was in a much more restricted sense.

---

51 Roosevelt 2019, 150–61.
52 Gauthier 1989, 151–70; Kosmin, 2019, 75–90.
53 Robert 1937, 155–58.
54 Payne and Wintjes 2016, 63–64.
55 Schmitt 2003.

Yet these developments also provide the background for the appearance of what Louis Robert called "un 'nationalisme lydien'" during the Roman imperial period.[56] Deities gain the epithet "Lydian," including the "Lydian Mother" (Μητὴρ θεῶν Λυδία) and Lydian Zeus, who is represented on Sardis' civic coinage, changes that may have much to do with the city's claim under Hadrian to be the "first metropolis" of Lydia.[57] Efforts were also made to cultivate a Lydian historical memory through the preservation of the palace of Croesus and the royal tumuli, along with other monuments and objects (*Lydiaka*, as Rojas has dubbed them) from the distant past.[58] At the same time, certain smaller communities began to identify as explicitly Lydian, such as Lydian Mostenê and Hermokapelia.[59]

This evidence has, for Spawforth, demonstrated the staying power of Lydian identity over more than half a millennium.[60] Yet surely it is no coincidence that expressions of Lydianness become most prominent under Roman rule. As suggested by Sardis' claim to be the metropolis of Lydia, the Romans encouraged competition among each region's major cities for status and recognition, and this was particularly acute in the highly urbanized province of Asia (Minor). Already under Tiberius, this competition was often expressed in terms of the antiquity of the city's history. Sardis, in striving for the honor of building a temple to the emperor, is said to have laid special emphasis on their kinship with the Etruscans, who they implied were the forefathers of all Italian peoples (Tac. *Ann.* 4.55). The persuasiveness of the argument is demonstrated by the fact that the Sardian claim was considered superior to all other claimants besides the winner, Smyrna, if Tacitus is to be believed. The cultivation of historical memory evoking a distant Lydian past was also monumentalized in a new inscription discovered in what was probably an imperial cult sanctuary, which recounts the history of the pre-Mermnad kings.[61] Clearly the drive to gain recognition from Rome motivated Sardis and probably other nearby communities to emphasize their Lydian credentials.

The upshot of these considerations is that the meaning, scope, and importance of the term Lydian changed over time. What was a powerful claim to empire (and an imperial capital) in the early sixth century BCE became an increasingly muted and limited identity under the Achaemenids, and then coalesced (again?) around Sardis in the Hellenistic period, broadening out

---

56   Robert 1982, 359–61.
57   Weiß 1995, 85–93.
58   Spawforth 2001, 384–92; Rojas 2013 and 2019, 35–43.
59   Robert 1976, 25–49; *TAM* V.2 1233.
60   Spawforth 2001.
61   Thonemann 2021. *Editio princeps*: Petzl 2019, nos. 577 and 578.

in a more regional (if still patchwork) sense under the Romans. This should make modern scholars cautious about employing the term as if it refers to a fixed group of people who naturally existed in a coherent way across time and throughout the region. Finally, there is one body of evidence that has yet to be explored: the presence of Lydians abroad, especially as they appear in Greek-language epigraphical evidence, especially in contexts that attracted immigrants like Athens, Delos, Rhodes, or the Hellenistic armies.[62] To what extent such espoused identities were the product of Lydian individuals themselves, as opposed to imposed ethnic categories familiar to Athenians and other host communities who enjoyed a sizable power advantage, especially when acting as masters to Lydian slaves, is a question worth investigating.

2.2   Mysians

It should come as no surprise that the Lydians' northern neighbors receive much less attention from scholars, since the best treatment is still a short article by Pierre Debord.[63] Such inattention goes back to Herodotos, who merely comments that Mysians were colonists (ἄποικοι) of the Lydians, likely agreeing with Xanthos (F15), and wore distinctive native armor (Hdt. 7.74). Subsequent authors such as Artemidoros seem to have debated the point, suggesting that the Mysians were colonists of Thracian Moesians from the northern Balkans (Strabo 7.3.2, 12.3.3; cf. 12.4.1, 12.8.3). The inspiration for this theory was Homer himself, who discusses the Mysians as living near the Thracians (*Iliad* 13.3–5). Strabo, in endorsing Artemidoros' theory, struggles to locate the boundaries of Mysia, which bleed into both Bithynia and Phrygia (12.4.4), and he identifies Mysians also in parts of Lydia, as we have seen. While Mysian settlement in Lydia could derive from later Attalid colonization, it may also date much earlier, as suggested by a hieroglyphic Luwian inscription from the late seventh century BCE, if the term *Musaza* refers to both Mysia and Lydia.[64] It is clear, in any case, that all of these sources represent external perspectives, which (with the exception of the Luwian text) valued Greek literary tradition over Mysian self-understanding.

While we know of no local historian of Mysia to counterbalance this etic viewpoint, we may be able to find traces of a local perspective in a few places. One is Herodotos' claim that Mysians, along with Lydians and Karians, had

---

62   The material for Athens and Delos can be found in the relevant *IG* volumes; the data on Rhodes has been usefully collected by Boyxen 2018. For foreigners in armies, see Launey 1949.
63   Debord 2001.
64   For this suggestion, see Hönigman and Oettinger 2018, 107.

access to the sanctuary of Zeus Karios at Mylasa, because Kar and Lydos and Mysos were brothers (1.171). Such a claim contradicts his earlier statement that Lydos' brother was Tyrrhenos (1.94) as well as his and Xanthos' assertion that Mysians were colonists of Lydians. The latter implies derivative and even subordinate status for the Mysians in relation to Lydians, while the idea that Mysos was Lydos' brother suggests equal and contemporary ethnic histories. Certainly, this story derives directly from a Karian source, but could also reflect a shared understanding with Mysians that placed these two ethnic communities on even footing with the Lydians in the face of a history of unequal relations due to Mermnad conquest and the administrative importance of Sardis under the Achaemenids.

The other source for a potentially Mysian perspective comes from the Attalid period. The Pergamene dynasts promoted visual propaganda that, especially on the Great Altar to Zeus on the Pergamene acropolis, vaunted the myth of Telephos as an important element in the dynasty's and city's identities.[65] Many scholars have focused on the 'Hellenizing' aspects of this myth, since it involves the migration of an Arkadian hero to Mysia, where he eventually becomes king.[66] Indeed, the story likely originated in earlier Greek literature.[67] Yet the myth also involves intermarriage with the local ruler, and an emphasis on Mysian history as Attalid/Pergamene history (cf. Strabo 12.8.4). The kingdom of Teuthrania serves as the setting and framing for the most important action, including Telephos' hostility toward the Achaeans on their way to Troy.[68]

In considering the relationship between this propaganda and a Mysian understanding of Mysian history, the crucial questions concern the origin of the myth and the audience for the propaganda. While the earliest evidence certainly comes from Greek language sources, what is harder to determine is where these sources derived their information. As Tanja Scheer has pointed out, the earliest sources for the Telephos myth (the Kypria epic cycle and Pindar) do not contain any reference to Arkadia, situating the hero and his deeds exclusively in Mysia.[69] And given that ethnography in the Archaic period was not organized or produced according to a Greek/non-Greek dichotomy, it is at least possible that the figure of Telephos reflected associations stemming from interaction between Greek and Mysian speakers.[70] This proposal must

---

65 Scheer 1993, 127, 134–47.
66 Hansen 1971, 5–6; Hall 1989, 174–76, 221–23; Stewart, 1996, 111; Seaman 2020, 58–62.
67 Scheer 1993, 74–86; Seaman 2020, 60–61. Cf. Lulli 2016, 50–68.
68 Kuttner 2005; Seaman 2020, 63–64. This imagery coexisted and overlapped with efforts to link the city's history with the Troad as well, on which see Kosmetatou 2001, 107–32.
69 Scheer 1993, 74.
70 For this view of early Greek ethnography, see Skinner 2012, 6–29.

remain speculative, but only if we acknowledge the same status for the idea that Greeks invented a history for Mysians *ex nihilo*.

Regardless of how we interpret this literary and visual evidence, what remains unclear is what institutions underlay the Mysian community. Unlike the Lydians, who as we have seen had a central city around which a broader identity could and did (at times) emerge, we know of no historical Mysian monarchy, major city or quintessentially 'Mysian' sanctuary.[71] The region seems to have been dominated by villages, some of which coalesced into larger communities (*koina*) that identified as specifically Mysian as early as the fifth century.[72] But until the Attalid dynasty the question of what impelled these communities to identify not just by the name of their *koinon* but also as Mysian remains unanswered. Pergamon, while clearly linked to Mysia, also fostered a distinct identity due to an influx of Macedonian settlers, as well as conceptual ties to its Aiolian neighbors.[73]

And yet, ironically, Mysians seem to have fostered a clearer sense of identity than Lydians in the Achaemenid and Hellenistic periods. Xenophon speaks of them frequently as a coherent group in his discussions Greek and Persian campaigns in the region.[74] One might think that this simply represented Xenophon's imposition of Greek ethnographic categories onto groups who identified in more local terms, and this is certainly possible, but epigraphic evidence from the Hellenistic period also shows groups and individuals identifying as Mysian in Mysia.[75] Some of this evidence suggests that the Attalid dynasty itself fostered military and administrative Mysian units around which Mysian identity could continue or coalesce.[76] Several inscriptions identify Mysians in military contexts, suggesting that the Attalids maintained specifically Mysian fighting units.[77] Military settlements of such units would have aided in the persistence of these identities, which continued well into the Roman period.[78]

---

71 Though see the suggestion (unconvincing to this author) of a Mysian kingdom in the late seventh and early sixth centuries BCE by Debord 2001, 140.

72 E.g., the Astyrenian Mysians attested in the Athenian Tribute Lists (*IG* I³ 268, 273). Cf. Debord 2001, 141–43. The institutional details of these larger communities escape us, so the term 'federation' is perhaps unsuitable.

73 Macedonians: Cohen 1995, 168–70. Aiolian ties: *IvP* I.245 (kinship with Pitane); cf. Curty 1995, 82–85.

74 For references and discussion, see Ma 2008.

75 Malay 1999, 96, 179 and 1990. It is important to stress this evidence as coming from Mysia, since individuals identifying as Mysian outside of Mysia had a greater chance of conforming to external (especially Greek) ethnic categories, particularly since in most contexts such individuals would have had less power (either as slaves or metics).

76 Debord 1985, 345–49.

77 *TAM* 5.444, 690.

78 Malay 1990; Naour 1981, 11–41.

The Attalid role in fostering a sense of Mysian community could mean that such a sense only developed during the Hellenistic period, but Xenophon's testimony possibly reflects more than his bias. Both he and the Oxyrynchos historian mention Mysians in the context of regional upheaval, and if John Ma is right that the Çan sarcophagos depicts a Mysian defeating a Persian enemy, this only strengthens the idea that Mysians maintained semi-autonomy under the Achaemenids by organizing into effective military groupings based on ethnic solidarity that served to transcend the extreme fragmentation of the village society.[79]

Other foundations for Mysian identity remain elusive. We know nothing helpful about the Mysian language, and Strabo's identification of Zeus Abretennos as "a Mysian god" probably does not mean that all Mysians worshiped him (12.8.9).[80] As with the Lydians, it would be beneficial to consider when and why individuals identified as Mysian outside of Mysia in immigrant or military service contexts.

2.3 Karians

As a native of Halikarnassos, Herodotos was especially well positioned to report on the Karians, which may explain the more helpful information he provides on this ethnic community. In addition to an origin story similar to those of the Lydians and Mysians – Karians are named after the eponymous Kar just as Lydians and Mysians recall Lydos and Mysos – he also shows what constituted the Karian *ethnos* in practice, namely participation in the cult of Zeus Karios at Mylasa (1.171). Interestingly, he adds that there are peoples who speak Karian but do not have a share in the cult, and thus are not Karian, revealing that language was not a marker of Karian identity.[81] In the next section, he implies that the Kaunians constituted one such group of non-Karian Karian-speakers.

Herodotos attributes his information to Karian sources, which he contrasts with the "Kretan" version that sees the Karians as migrants into the region from the Aegean islands, and there are good reasons to believe him about his sources. Besides his upbringing in close proximity to Mylasa and other Karian

---

79   *Hell. Oxy.* 16.1; Ma 2008.
80   The language of the inscription found on the edge of Mysia remains unidentified: Cox and Cameron 1932, 34–49. Xanthos of Lydia's remark (F8) that the Mysians speak *mixolydion* could equally refer to Mysian as related to Lydian but with loanwords from Phrygian (so Hönigman and Oettinger 2018, 108), or to Mysian as an unrelated language with loanwords from Lydian.
81   Herodotos' language here makes clear that the main target of exclusion from the sanctuary are Karian-speakers who are not Karian, rather than Greeks, as argued by Bachvarova 2013, 154–55.

communities, there is the fact that he endorses the Kretan version, against which it would be counterproductive to invent the Karian point of view.[82] Finally, the Karian version relates to Xanthos' version of Lydian origins discussed above, but with an important difference. The Karians linked themselves to Lydians through the siblings Kar and Lydos, but just as in the case of Mysos, in an equal relationship, rather than what Xanthos propagated in casting Mysians as a Lydian colony.

Unlike the Lydians, Herodotos' Karians were not united politically under a monarchy, and yet they were capable of concerted political action during the so-called Ionian Revolt. As allies in the revolt, the Karians engaged in several battles with the Persian forces, including one victory, and assembled to discuss strategy (5.88, 5.119.2). Hornblower takes this as evidence that the Karian League attested in later periods already existed at the end of the sixth century.[83] Others have suggested its creation under the Hekatomnids, focusing on the more direct evidence from later inscriptions, two fourth-century and one second-century.[84] Of the first two, one shows the Karians sending a delegation to the Persian king, while the other refers to a "king of the Karians," a title repeated in the second-inscription and clarified with the addition of "priest."[85]

The Karians thus enjoyed institutions to enforce their collective ethnic identity at least by the fourth-century, if not sooner. Both Hornblower and Carstens see the Hekatomnid period as a key moment in the "Karianization" of the region, whereby the dynasts constructed a common Karian identity for their subjects not only via institutions like the Karian League, but also through the development of a regionally distinct cultural style in monuments like the Maussolleion and the temple to Zeus at Labraunda, involving hybridized artistic and architectural forms drawing on local, Greek, and Persian traditions.[86]

We will explore the cultural aspects of this view of Karian identity below, but here it is important to observe that, institutionally speaking, it is problematic to view the Hekatomnids as an unprecedented and quintessentially Karian dynasty. One reason is that the domains of the satrap-dynasts were always multi-ethnic, encompassing both Karians and Greeks, and eventually

---

82   The Kretan sources seem to have also influenced Thucydides (3.104), who allowed this tale to color his interpretation of the Geometric burials that the Athenians dug up on Delos. Cf. Brock 1996.
83   Hornblower 1982, 55–62; followed by Carstens 2009, 78–80.
84   Debord 2003, 118–25; Capdetrey 2007, 95–96, 104–05. Cf. Capdetrey 2012.
85   *SIG*³ 167; *IMylasa* 106; 828. Cf. Laumonier 1958, 42–43; Robert 1937, 571 and n.2. For a possible additional reference to a Hekatomnid as a king of Karia, see Maddoli 2010, 127–28 and Nafissi 2015.
86   Hornblower 1982, 276 and 352; Carstens 2009, 2013. Cf. Henry 2013a.

Lykians. More importantly, the Karians' capacity for collective action seems to have been connected politically to the Persian administration, since we find the Karians acting separately from Maussollos in sending a delegation to the Persian king – one member of the delegation even conspiring against him. This suggests a Persian-supported institution that may have strengthened Karian identity, but whose impetus and origins may lie beyond (and possibly before) the dynasty.[87] At the same time, the league was defined more in terms of religious functions that bound the community together, since the "king of the Karians" was exclusively a religious office by the Hellenistic period, and probably sooner.[88] We unfortunately do not know much else about the league's functioning, such as how frequently member communities met or who was included and excluded. But given the importance of religion to the Karian community in Herodotos' day, it seems likely that the religious functions of the league date to the fifth century.

The other relevant institution that reinforced Karian identity was a Hellenistic development known as the Chrysaorean League. This federation emerged by the second quarter of the third century as a religious coalition of at least seven cities in Karia, whose members worshiped Zeus Chrysaoros and at times chose to self-identify abroad as "Chrysaoreans."[89] While Chrysaoreans represented a subset of the larger Karian ethnic group, as confirmed by an inscription from Labraunda referring to "Chrysaoreans or other Karians," they also constituted their own ethnic group, or *ethnos* according to an Amphiktyonic decree, whose commonality was based on descent from Chrysaor, a figure associated with Kar and Bellerophon, in addition to the regional storm god (Zeus Chrysaoros).[90] By Strabo's day, the equivalence with Karians was strong enough that he could misrepresent the league as existing for all Karians (14.2.25).

---

87   Klinkott 2009, 2015; LaBuff 2017.
88   LaBuff forthcoming, countering the views of Hornblower 1982 (55–62), Debord 2003 (118–25), and Capdetrey 2012 that the league continued to have a political function in the Hellenistic period. Cf. Parker 2018, 37, doubting the existence of the league until the second century.
89   Hornblower 1982, 62–63; Debord 1994; 2003, 130–42; Lozano Velilla 2006, 373–80. Gabrielsen (2011) argues that the league also served a political function, countered by LaBuff forthcoming. Debate also exists over whether the league was a creation of Maussollos (Hornblower) or the Ptolemies (Debord and Lozano Velilla, followed by Capdetrey 2007, 106–08), or was established by its member cities (Gabrielsen and LaBuff).
90   Labraunda inscription: *Labraunda* 5, lines 15–16; Amphikytonic decree: FD III.4.163, lines 11–13. For the associations with Kar and Bellerophon, see LaBuff forthcoming, n. 36; Sauzeau 1997; Debord 2010.

At this point it is worth noting that known members of the Chrysaorean League, and at least the focal point of the Karian League (since we lack any specifics on which communities belonged), were all situated in the western half of the geographical region of Karia. What this means for the ethnic identity of inhabitants of eastern Karia, until communities like Aphrodisias begin fostering kinship and shared historical memory with west Karian communities in the imperial period, remains unclear.[91] Strabo himself struggles to locate the boundaries of the Karian community, similarly to his portrayal of Lydians and Mysians. Not only does he find Karians among other peoples north of the Maeander River, a river he claims constitutes the northern limit of Karia, but he seems to exclude communities to the east, including Aphrodisias which were even part of the Roman administrative unit in his day.[92] Again it is unclear what the geographer's criteria were for determining who was Karian, but he seems to employ two meanings of the term, one etic in conception that externally identified Karians both in and outside of Karia, and the other quasi-emic that focused on membership in the Chrysaorean League and thus on the western communities in the region. Since nothing in our evidence suggests that any Karians outside Karia were involved in the league, it is possible that Strabo's claim that all Karians participated in it stemmed from a local source that had a more restricted understanding of the Karian ethnic community. If so, then this would mean that by the late first century the original Karian League was defunct.

The coexistence of two ethnic federations in the Hellenistic period may be explained in two ways. I suggest elsewhere that Chrysaorean identity allowed some Karians to express their distinctiveness abroad without the negative associations that Greeks ascribed to Karians.[93] In addition, this development may also be tied to the expansion of what it meant to be Karian at this time. Later evidence suggests that communities from eastern Karia developed notions of kinship with the original 'core' of Karian communities that belonged to the Chrysaorean League.[94] If these eastern communities were not part of the Chrysaorean League – we cannot assume that confirmed examples represent all members – then such kinship ties may have formed the basis for a broader Karian identity that had come to align with Roman (and possibly Seleukid) administrative categories.

---

91 E.g., *MAMA* VIII 418b.
92 13.4.12, 14.1.38, 42. Fabiani 2000, 373–400.
93 LaBuff forthcoming.
94 E.g., Panamara and Nysa (*IStratonikeia* 27).

As with the Lydians, it is also common to assume that language and names served to express Karian identity.[95] Unlike Lydian, the Karian language was being written at least as early as the seventh century BCE, but early texts come largely from Egypt, where the vast majority of our surviving documents have been found. Only about a fifth of the extant texts come from Karia itself and the majority of these hail from the fourth century and from the areas around Mylasa, Stratonikeia, and Kaunos.[96] This could suggest a process in which Karian linguistic difference in Egypt reinforced, or even led to, Karian identity, which filtered back to Karia itself, where writing in Karian peaked in the fourth century just when interactions with another ethnic Other, the Greeks, were intensifying.[97] There is, however, Herodotos' denial of language as a marker of Karian identity (see above), which seems confirmed by the diversity of alphabetic traditions across the region.[98] In particular, the Kaunian variant is the predominant form in the Egyptian texts, a fact that problematizes the desire to see Egypt as a place of Karian ethnogenesis, since at least until Herodotos' own day Kaunians did not perceive themselves as Karian. Moreover, Karians were writing in Greek around the same time as they were writing in Karian; bilingualism, at least among the literate few, was the order of the day precisely when Karian writing was most common. This situation of multilingualism, which may lie behind the claim by the local historian Philip of Theangela that the language had a plethora of loan words from Greek (*FGrH* 741 F1), would have further weakened the association between language and ethnic identity.[99]

A similar debate plays out regarding the onomastic evidence. Linguistically Karian personal and place names predominate in central Karia, leading scholars to draw several conclusions: that the preservation of such names implied the retention of a Karian identity in the face of Greek culture; that where one finds such names outside Karia proper, this provides evidence of Karians; and that, in a city like Halikarnassos where such names abound, they suggest the ethnically mixed nature of the community.[100] Yet the onomastic evidence

---

95   Robert 1937, 337–39; Hornblower 1982, 341–50; Bresson 2007a, 217–28; Piras 2009; Adiego 2013; Waelkens 2013; Saviano 2017.
96   Adiego 2007, 128–63. Cf. Piras 2009, 230–31 & 2010, 244–48; Adiego 2013.
97   This is the view of Piras 2010, 217–21, though without a link to the Egyptian evidence. Adiego (2019, 24–26) has recently linked an archaic graffito on a potsherd found near Mylasa with the Egyptian script, but also notes that this graffito differs from the alphabet used in fourth-century Mylasa.
98   On which, see Adiego 2007, 205–33; 2013, 19–20.
99   Cf. LaBuff 2013, 86–97; Unwin 2019. Philip is typically assigned to the third or second centuries BCE.
100   Aubriet 2013; Hornblower 1982, 346–50. This conclusion is often restated, especially in discussions of Herodotos' own identity.

from Halikarnassos, which refers only to the common Halikarnassian identity of all individuals, whether they bear a Greek or Karian name, can also be read in the opposite way, i.e., as showing that the linguistic origin of names did not express ethnic identity.[101] The continued popularity of "Hekatomnid" names well into the Hellenistic and even Roman periods has also been taken to indicate a collective Karian pride in their glorious past.[102] Yet more work needs to be done on this evidence to determine where and among which social groups such names were popular, before assuming that such names spoke to ethnic rather than local or class identity.

As we have seen, the argument that the Hekatomnids oversaw the crystallization of Karian identity depends largely on that identity being based on a common architectural and artistic style as expressed in religious and funerary monuments. Certainly, even before the fourth century, cultic life played a central role in perpetuating Karian (and eventually, Chrysaorean) identity, through the cults of Zeus Karios, Zeus Panamareus, and Zeus Chrysaoros. Efforts have also been made to identify other aspects of religion that may have reinforced

---

[101] LaBuff 2013, 97–99. This claim relates to attempts to locate a 'Karian' element in the city histories of Halikarnassos and Miletos. In the former case, such an interpretation depends on readings of the recently discovered Salmakis inscription, which recounts the origins of Halikarnassos as a series of foundations, including the rearing of Zeus by the *gêgeneis* (earth-born) and settlers led by Bellerophon well before the arrival of 'Greek' settlers from Athens and Troizen (Isager 1998; Gagné 2006; Bremmer 2009, 2013; D'Alessio 2004; Isager 2004; Jones 1999; Santini 2016, 2017; McInerney 2020). Concerning Miletos, discussion revolves around Herodotos' account of the founding of the city through forced marriage with Karian women (after killing their husbands), along with Herakleides' tale of a civil conflict between wealthy Milesians and the *demos*, who were called Gergithes. This name's non-Greek linguistic status has spawned suppositions of class divisions based on ethnic (Greek-Karian) and geographic lines (city-*chora*): Faraguna 1995 and Zurbach 2019; *contra* Gorman 2009. In both cases, the label 'Karian' is usually imposed and accompanied by an implicit faith in our often late literary evidence. The Salmakis inscription's avoidance of the term Karian has been taken as the result of a need to mute this aspect of Halikarnassos' past, but it could also stem from the relative unimportance of regional identities or of ethnic binaries. The Milesian stories also push past these binaries: the point of Herodotos' tale is to stress that all Milesians are part-Karian, while the Gergithes are represented as a subset of the Milesian civic body – their existence in the countryside depends on a lemma in the *Suda* that refers to the wealthy Milesians as those ἐν περιβολῇ, a phrase not common for distinguishing urban and rural spaces, who are contrasted with the Gergithes described as ἡ τύρβη καὶ οἱ χειρώνακτες, words which evoke a dense population involve in an urban economy. In any case, the credibility of this entry, or at least an explanation of why its crucial information is not in any other earlier source, remains wanting.

[102] Bresson 2007a, 226.

this identity.[103] Certain cults seem to have enjoyed regional importance with or without explicit reference to the Karians, such as Zeus Labraundos, which was the site of a dispute between the local priesthood and the city of Mylasa in the second half of the third century, and Hekate at Lagina, home to an impressive sculptural program that seems to depict a series of Karian communities.[104] On the other hand, these sanctuaries also played a vital role in cementing new and evolving urban identities.[105] Moreover, Debord's investigation of a possible Karian "pantheon" leads him to conclude that the region's religious landscape was defined by difference rather than unity.[106]

On a related note, the sacred architecture at sites like Labraunda and the sanctuary of Artemis at Amyzon has been interpreted as promoting a uniquely Karian style that enacted Karian historical memory.[107] Similar conclusions have been drawn about aspects of the Maussolleion.[108] One study has even sought to distinguish Karians from Ionians in the Early Iron Age through distinct ceramic styles.[109] Yet all of these proposals are dubious, as the arguments are inevitably circular.[110] The temples and the Maussolleion are both the product of the Hekatomnid dynasts, who are seen to create or disseminate a Karian identity through these monuments only because their Karian identity is assumed to be significant in the first place. Others have noted that the styles employed in these monuments contributed to the dynasts' political ambitions by speaking to Persian idioms of power.[111] Indeed, one has to wonder how many Karians would have shared our bird's-eye view of stylistic differences, which depend on a transregional set of comparisons that few ancients would have been interested in or able to pursue.

Burial practice is another candidate for Karian identity expression. In particular, the form and location of the chamber-tombs in the region are seen as an expression of Karian culture.[112] Yet the similarities with Lykian tombs complicates this interpretation.[113] To what extent these traditions operated to establish differences at the local level to reinforce social distinctions between

---

103 Foundational in this regard is Laumonier 1958. Cf. Carstens 2009, 23–26.
104 Labraunda: Carstens 2009, 75–100; Hekate: Nilsson 1906, 397–98; Robert 1937, 552–55; more cautiously, Webb 1996, 108–20; Parker 2000, 69–70. Cf. Debord 2013.
105 Williamson 2021.
106 Debord 2009, 251–65.
107 Hellström 2009, 267–90; cf. Bokisch et al. 2013, 129–62.
108 Prost 2013, 175–86; Carstens 2009, 37–74.
109 Herda and Sauter 2009; cf. Benda-Weber 2005, 217–42.
110 Cf. Carstens 2009, 102–03.
111 E.g., Karlsson 2013.
112 Voigtländer 1989; Henry 2013b.
113 Henry 2010, 115–22; Dusinberre 2013, 201–05.

elites and non-elites, as opposed to differences at the transregional level to highlight ethnic distinctions between Karians (*cum* Lykians?) and neighboring groups like Greeks and Lydians, remains unclear. In considering all these cultural forms, the rejection of a single, homogenous Karian culture and the acknowledgement of key similarities with East Greeks, are, to this author, more sensible conclusions.[114]

To summarize, the Karian ethnic group was fully developed by the fifth century, if not earlier, and persisted well into the Hellenistic and Roman periods. Yet the sparse evidence for ethnic institutions also reminds us that the growth of autonomous local communities from the fourth century represented a rival identity, rather than just a subset, that diminished the importance of Karian and Chrysaorean allegiance in the realm of politics. These communities, which included both *poleis* and groupings of villages called *koina*, published far more expressions of collective identity in our surviving evidence, which led to far more individuals identifying by their civic ethnic over a federal ethnic like "Chrysaorean."[115]

2.4 *Lykians*

Herodotos' Lykian *logos* appears far less credible than his ethnography of the Karians (1.173). Not only does his claim that the Lykians were a matrilineal society find no corroboration in the epigraphic evidence from the region, but he implies that his sources were all external.[116] His account of the origin of the Lykians sounds suspiciously like the Cretan version of the origin of the Karians, though with the specification that the Lykians came from Crete under the leadership of Sarpedon, brother of Minos.[117] Meanwhile, he correctly observes that the native word for "Lykians" is Termilai (Lyk. *trmmili*), but attributes its usage not to the Lykians themselves but to their neighbors. Given that the Persians referred to Lykians by a variant of this name (*Turmiyap*), it is likely that he mistook their imperial terminology for an externally imposed label, which suggests that he never spoke to any Lykians directly.[118]

The sources for Homer's reports on the Lykians are even murkier. In the *Iliad*, the Lykians not only feature in the Catalogue of Ships, but are the subject of the exchange between Diomedes and Glaukos that relates the story of Bellerophon (6.119–236). Herodotos is clearly indebted to this tradition in his

---

114 Debord 2004, 365–68; Bresson 2007a, 213–15; Henry 2013a, 6–8; Rumscheid 2019; Aytaçları 2019.
115 On *koina* in general, see LaBuff 2016, 4–5 and 136–37, with references.
116 Prost 2007, 108.
117 This tradition is perpetuated by later authors, as discussed in Keen 1998, 22–26.
118 On Persian and other West Asian terms for Lykians, see Schmitt 2003.

focus on Sarpedon, the leader of the Lykian forces at Troy, and in his preference for the term 'Lykian' itself. Both authors also associate Lykians with the western end of what is geographically understood as Lykia, and with the city of Xanthos in particular (Hdt. 1.176).[119] In Herodotos' case, we can connect this to an Athenian imperial understanding of the region, since the tribute lists link 'Lykians' with Telmessos, the only specifically named community in the region.[120]

Fortunately, there is evidence that shines a light onto Lykian understandings of themselves. First, the Homeric tradition was adopted by at least some Lykian individuals and communities, as the depiction of Bellerophon on a funerary monument and the naming of a Xanthian tribe after Sarpedon shows. But it is quite an exaggeration to surmise from these cases that the Lykians had "totally integrated" this tradition.[121] At the same time, several fragmentary histories survive that link various regional communities together through ancestral ties, including Menekrates of Xanthos in the fourth century BCE (*FGrH* 769). In one fragment, he portrays his native city as colonizing Pinaros and Mount Kragos in western Lykia (F1). An earlier variant is reported by Panyassis of Halikarnassos, in which the eponymous ancestor Tremiles begets Tlos, Xanthos, Pinaros, and Kragos (fr. 18 Kinkel), a version could go back to Hekataios, who discusses Lykians and Tremiles in the *Genealogies* (*FGrH* 1 F10).[122] Since Hekataios sought to correct the "silly stories" of the Greeks (F1), it is at least possible that in this case he did so by consulting local sources. In any case, Panyassis' genealogy shows up again in the Hellenistic historians Polycharmos (*FGrH* 770 F5) and Alexander Polyhistor (*FGrH* 273 F58) and was endorsed by several Lykian communities in the Imperial period.[123] The discrepancy between Menekrates and our other sources can easily be explained by his desire to promote the political dominance of Xanthos.[124] The important point is that by the fourth century, if not earlier, there is good reason to believe that western Lykian communities had begun to define their commonality in terms of common descent, whether this belief was originally developed locally or borrowed from ethnographies in Greek.

---

119   Cf. Bryce 1986, 23–40.
120   Bryce 1986, 100–101. Note also that Herodotos attributes the name of the Lykians to an Athenian migration or colonization of the region under Lykos son of Pandion (1.173).
121   Le Roy 2004, 8, for the quote and references. He later shows (8–11) that such integration only occurred by the Roman period.
122   Cf. Huxley 1964, 29–33.
123   *TAM* II.174, 555. Cf. Weiß 1984, 189; Jones 1999, 144–50.
124   Jenkins 2016.

With Lykia we are also fortunate to possess the largest epigraphic corpus of any Anatolian language from the Iron Age, which has permitted a much greater level of decipherment of both script and language than other languages on the peninsula (Greek and Aramaic excepted). This evidence has not only confirmed the Lykian word for 'Lykian,' as we have seen, but also shown that some of the earliest uses of *trmmili* come from Xanthos, and in particular its dynasts.[125] The famous inscribed pillar from the late fifth century uses it several times, matching the short epigram in Greek that explicitly mentions Lykians twice.[126] This, in combination with the perspectives of Homer, Herodotos and the Athenian Tribute Lists – which record the Lykians in conjunction with Telmessos – has led to broad consensus that Lykian identity was based in the Xanthos valley by the end of the Archaic period.[127] Difference of opinion centers on whether this identity encompassed the entire region at this time, minus the northern uplands and the Elmalı plain, or spread to central and eastern Lykia only by the fourth century.[128]

The issue is complicated first by the use of *trmmili* in eastern Lykia, where it most often appears in the context of the poorly understood *itlehi trmmili*. This phrase has been variously translated as Lykian gods, heroes, a disciplinary authority or office, or even as a political league.[129] We will return to the meaning of the phrase below, but the important point here is that an explicitly Lykian institution existed only in central and eastern Lykia, but not in the west, the supposed heart of Lykia, suggesting important regional variation rather than a spread from west to east.[130] If *itlehi* refers to gods or heroes, then these Lykian objects of worship were not revered by all Lykians. If it refers to a social or political institution, then the very meaning of *trmmili* varied across the region, referring only to some 'Lykians' of eastern and central Lykia for the inhabitants of these areas.

To resolve the problem, it may help to ask what was driving Lykian ethnic identity during the late Classical period, when most Lykian texts were written. Geographically speaking, the region was divided into three major zones based on the three major river valleys of the Xanthos, the Myros, and the

---

125 Prost 2007, 107–08.
126 *TL* 44. Cf. Bousquet 1992, 155–88.
127 *IG* I³ 266, col. III.2, lines 33–34; cf. Diodoros 11.60.4.
128 Whole region: Bryce 1986, 99–103. Later spread: Frei 1993, 95–97; Potter 2007. Cf. Zimmermann 1992, 27–51. On the exclusion of northern Lykia, see Coulton 1993, 79–85; Keen 1998, 30–31.
129 Bryce 1986, 135–36. Tribunal: Le Roy 2005, 335–40. Federation: Carruba 1996, 211–25; cf. Borchhardt 2003.
130 Kolb 2018, 79.

Arykandos-Limyros. The mountains separating these areas could be bypassed via the sea, which likely explains the southern orientation of similarities in language and material culture in the region.[131] Politically, we do not know much until the Persian period, when a series of dynasties emerge, best attested by the coins minted by these dynasts. What is unclear is whether these dynasts ruled contemporarily, and if so, whether there was a hierarchy that subordinated all other dynasts to a 'king' of Lykia based at Xanthos. The coins themselves cannot completely resolve this question, but differences in weight between issues in the west and center-east could suggest political fragmentation from the mid-fifth century, and unity prior.[132]

One perspective that did conceptualize the entire region as ethnically monolithic was that of the Achaemenids, who not only used a single ethnic label for Lykians, as we have seen, but also administratively defined the region as a "Termilian satrapy," at least by the late fifth century (*TL* 44b, line 26). The reference to this satrapy in the inscribed pillar of Xanthos seems to have acted as an aspirational goal for the Xanthian dynasts, who sought to expand their holdings by conquering neighboring cities, motivating their very decision to define their power and identity as Termilian and (in Greek) Lykian. Whether or not this aspiration hearkens back to an earlier time when the Xanthian dynasts controlled the whole region as Persian vassals, it raises the possibility that Lykian identity was forged in the context of membership in an empire that, as we have discussed with regard to the Lydians and Karians, understood its subjects in terms of broad ethnic categories. This possibility would also account for the limited scope of the *itlehi*, since local but trans-communal institutions were not beholden to apply to all communities within the Persian imperial construct of Lykia, while still finding that construct useful. At the same time, the 'nationalistic' propaganda of the Xanthian dynasts, as well as that of Perikles of Limyra, who was more successful in conquering the entire region, would have reinforced the Persian-inspired understanding of Lykia not simply as an administrative unit, but as an ethnic collective.[133]

There is also the possibility that some Lykian communities together formed a political federation in the Classical period. The argument for this possibility largely depends on linking the legend ITE on certain coin issues with the aforementioned *itlehi trmmili*, which would mean something like "federated Lykians."[134] But beyond the speculation involved in translating either of these

---

131 Bresson 2007b, 73–74; Schweyer 1996, 3–68.
132 Mørkholm & Zahle 1972 and 1976. Cf. Hoff 2017, 423–24.
133 On Perikles, see Wörrle 1991, 202–39.
134 Carruba 1996.

terms, there seems to be no precedent for any federation minting coins with the word "league" only on it, rather than the identity of that league. Along similar lines, the heavier minting standard and prevalence of the *triskeles* symbol on coins from central and eastern Lykia have been tentatively suggested to indicate a federation.[135] It seems difficult to move beyond speculation here. The fact that Aristotle composed a *Politeia Lukiôn* (fr. 548) is less helpful than it might appear, since he also grouped the politically fragmented regions of Cyprus and Crete into single works on the *politeia of* each island.[136]

Regardless, an imperial institutional basis for Lykian identity may have survived the fall of the Achaemenid Empire, since for much of the third century the Ptolemies controlled all of southern Lykia and possibly ruled the region through a Lykiarch.[137] A decree from this period issued by the city of Limyra indicates that Ptolemaic benefaction was understood to fall upon the Lykians as a group.[138] This context serves to explain the continuity between the frequent use of *trmmili* or *Lukioi* in the fourth century and the creation of a formal Lykian League in the second century, which aimed to establish a regional polity free from Rhodian control in the wake of the Peace of Apamea. In this aim, the league was ultimately successful, and its membership over the next two centuries helped to redefine Lykian identity, which now contained an overtly political element, to include additional communities in the east, such as Phaselis, and in the northern highlands.[139] Such institutional foundations and continuity help explain why individuals from the region identified as "Lykian" rather than or in addition to their city ethnics much more frequently than other Anatolians, a pattern that continued well into the Roman period, thanks in large part to the maintenance of the *koinon* as a Roman imperial institution after the region was incorporated into the provincial administration.[140]

Beyond this institutionally based identity, it is typical to assume an inherent link between Lykian identity and language. Lykian language texts dominate in the region from the late fifth to the end of the fourth century, leading many to see this as a clear expression of ethnic identity.[141] Unlike Karian, Lykian texts show little alphabetic or dialectical variation, with the exception of three inscriptions in 'Lykian B,' which was either a poetic sacred variant or

---

135 Mørkholm & Zahle 1972, 79–82, 113; Hoff 2017, 423–24. Contra: Behrwald 2000, 22–39.
136 Cf. Kolb 2018, 77.
137 Behrwald 2000, 46–80; cf. Wörrle 1978.
138 Wörrle 1977.
139 Behrwald 2000, 89–159; Schuler 2016. This inclusion, however, was not always permanent.
140 Mitchell 2000, 122–23; cf. Syme 1995, 270–85.
141 Frei 1993; Bresson 2007b; Potter 2007; Prost 2007; Schürr 2013; Waelkens 2013; Hoff 2017, 1–3, 9–12, 34–35, 341–48.

represented a dialect peculiar to south-central Lykia.[142] While Greek script and language was not as prominent, it was written in the region even earlier than Lykian itself, and continued to serve as another means of communication by Lykian elites during the fifth and fourth centuries, leading some scholars to question the link between ethnicity and script, if not language.[143] Certainly by the second century BCE, as the Lykian League rose to prominence, the use of Greek was not seen as contradictory to the centrality of Lykian identity within the federation. The same can be said for linguistically Lykian names, which coexist with Greek names within the same social milieu, or even in the same person, from the fifth century on.[144]

In the realm of material culture, sculptural and architectural style and architecture in funerary monuments have been said to have had a distinctly Lykian flavor that conveyed ethnic identity. The combination of Greek, Persian, Anatolian, and Levantine styles in the iconography of dynastic and elite funerary monuments is supposed to have created a Lykian identity.[145] Others have pointed out the difficulty of connecting perceived cultural unity to a specific ethnic milieu.[146] What appears uniquely 'Lykian' to us, i.e., what is distinct in form and iconography from other regions of the Mediterranean and West Asia, was not necessarily understood in those terms by the producers and viewers of these monuments. What is clear is that power and status were inherent to the stylistic and content choices being made, which linked elite Lykians more with neighboring elites and differentiated them from the majority of 'Lykians.' Here the target audience is important to keep in mind: local and regional inhabitants would have been much more likely to visually experience these monuments (and for other elites, read the few inscribed ones) than foreigners, given the rural context of most and the extremely rare presence of Greek.

Finally, the role of religion in fostering Lykian identity should be considered. The notion of a Lykian 'pantheon' is a modern scholarly construct based on regionally widespread cults to Zeus, Apollo, and Artemis, which do not correspond to expressions of ethnic commonality in our evidence.[147] The sanctuary of the Letoön near Xanthos probably functioned as a pan-Lykian

---

142   Most scholars favor the former interpretation (see Kolb 2018, 80). For the latter, see Schürr 2001.
143   Kolb 2018, 81–83 still assumes that (spoken) language was an expression of Lykian identity, but questions the use of the script for this function. Payne 2006 is more cautious, pointing to the function of both languages as expressions of power.
144   Colvin 2004; Schürr 2007. *Contra* Bryce 1990, 535–41.
145   Coles-Rannous 2013. Cf. Akurgal 1993; Prost 2007, 108–11.; Hoff 2017, 1–12. Less unequivocally: Dusinberre 2013, 189–201.
146   Frei 1993, 95–96.
147   N. Şahın 2016. Cf. Frei 1990.

cult, but not as prominently as one might expect; only one League decree has been found at the site and the only attested federal priest managed the cult of Apollo Patroios at Patara.[148] This perhaps explains why league coinage features a male bust rather than Leto.[149] But studies of these sanctuaries have not yet addressed the question of who was visiting the Letoön or the cult of Apollo Patroios (if it was not a league creation) in earlier centuries, apart from local inhabitants of Xanthos and Patara.[150] There are also widespread reliefs in Roman Lykia depicting twelve hunter gods which are, in one case, specifically called "Lykian," but while the content of these depictions can be linked to Bronze Age Hittite reliefs, no clear parallels exist with anything from earlier periods in Lykia itself.[151] This regionally shared cultic practice thus was only recognized as distinctly Lykian under the Romans.[152]

Lykian identity thus seems to have been driven especially by political considerations, both in negotiation with empire (Persian, Ptolemaic, Roman) and emanating from the ambitions of individual dynasts and, eventually, autonomy-seeking communities. External Greek understandings of Lykians could be influential as well, but only insofar as they spoke to these broader considerations.

2.5 *Bithynians*

Herodotos first refers to Bithynians as the Thracians in Asia (3.90). Later, he admits that they called themselves Bithynians, and had migrated from around the Strymon River in the northern Balkans due to pressure from Mysians and Teucrians (7.75). Interestingly, these are the only "Thracians" he lists as regular contingents in the Persian invading army, although many Balkan tribes were conscripted as the force advanced southward toward the resisting Greeks (7.110). In calling the Bithynians Thracian, Herodotos is likely following Achaemenid imperial categories, which used the term *Skudra* without further distinction when referring to this part of their realm. Strabo's account adds, citing Skylax (F11) and several other authors, that the Bithynians resulted from the mixture of Mysians and Thracian newcomers (12.3.3; 12.4.8).

---

148 Behrwald 2000, 182–87; C. Le Roy 2004, 11–15; Ashton and Meadows 2008; Laroche 2007, 169–74. On the league document at the Letoön, see Rousset 2010. Le Roy 1996. On the priest of Apollo Patroios, see *OGIS* 565 and *TAM* II.247, 905.
149 Behrwald 2000, 99–105.
150 On the Letoön, see Hansen and Le Roy 2012 and 1976; Le Roy 1991. Study of the sanctuary of Apollo Patroios before the Roman period is almost non-existent, but the cult may be linked to the mountain oracle mentioned in Herodotos (1.182); cf. Raimond 2002.
151 Drew-Bear and Labarre 2004; Renberg 2014.
152 Raimond 2009 attempts to identify distinctly Lykian and Solymean pantheons under the misguided and unproven assumption that that ancient religion was based in theology rather than practice.

This literary evidence has led to general acceptance among the few scholars working on Bithynian identity, some of whom even prefer to call them Thracian.[153] Yet we may wish to take a more critical approach to these external perspectives. Herodotos' account suggests that Bithynians did not call themselves Thracians; even when they lived in Thrace they called themselves Strymonians. Thus, it appears that Herodotos, possibly following the Persians but almost certainly as a result of the slave trade, imposed a constructed category of 'Thracian' that lumped different communities together, presumably based on similarities that he perceived but that may not have mattered to the communities themselves, as the prominence of 'tribal' names in his account suggests.[154] Meanwhile, Strabo grounds his arguments on the authority of earlier authors who refer to certain locales in Bithynia as "Mysian," and to certain tribes in Thrace called Thynians and (supposedly) Bithynians. The logic here involves connecting geographical 'dots' from a distance, an exercise that does not seem to have been undertaken by the Bithynians (or 'Thracians') themselves.

From an institutional vantage point, the emergence of a Bithynian dynasty under the Persians was crucial to fostering Bithynian identity. As is well known, these rulers succeeded in establishing a fully independent kingdom by the third century BCE.[155] Their power seems to have depended on a healthy relationship with the local warrior aristocracy, who held high-ranking military and administrative posts and were granted land in the kings' expanding territories.[156] At least some rulers identified as "King of the Bithynians" explicitly in diplomatic contexts.[157]

Unfortunately, beyond these general points, it is difficult to know if the kings fostered an explicitly ethnic ideology or political mythology in communicating with their Bithynian subjects. The closest sign of this is the growth of local Bithynian historiography in the Hellenistic period, through the stylus of authors like Demosthenes of Bithynia. Their relationship to the Bithynian rulers is, however, uncertain, and what little survives from their works focuses on the history of the various cities of the region, rather than on the Bithynian *ethnos* as a whole. Only in the Roman period does Arrian address this latter topic in the form of a genealogy in which the eponymous ancestor Bithynos hails either from Zeus and the nymph Thrakê, or from Odryses, and becomes the

---

153   Corsten 2007, 121; Michels 2009, 12–14.
154   On the role of slavery in informing ethnographic perceptions of Thracians and other non-Greek groups in Athens in particular, see Xydopoulos 2007; Harrison 2019.
155   Vitucci 1953, 130–31; Scholten 2007; Gabelko 2017, 319–24.
156   Corsten 2007; Gabelko 2017, 329–30.
157   *IG* XII.4.1 209; cf. the heavily restored Reynolds and Erim 1982, #4.

adopted brother of Paphlagon (*FGrH* 156 F77a).[158] But it is unclear when and in what context such mythic ties with neighboring peoples were formulated and articulated before Arrian, or to what extent he was conveying internal or outside traditions.

How ancient writers, whether local or Greek outsiders, identified Bithynians also remains unknown. Strabo intimates the difficulty of distinguishing among Bithynians, Mysians, and Phrygians along the borders of Bithynia, but not why (12.4.4). Modern commentators, meanwhile, focus above all on language distinction. The only written language in the region is Greek, so it is the onomastic evidence alone that suggests a non-Greek linguistic tradition, making it impossible to determine whether Bithynians spoke a different language or dialect from Thracian. Alongside notes of caution, the presence of 'Thraco-Bithynian' names in the epigraphic evidence is generally taken to indicate the existence of Bithynians both on the wealthy landed estates of the countryside and in the dynastic foundations (or refoundations) of Nikomedeia, Prousa, Nikaia, et al.[159] The approach is imperfect, above all because a linguistically Greek name does not guarantee that its bearer did not identify as Bithynian, but it does allow us to draw conclusions in the realm of probability. What it cannot do is indicate the role of the Bithynian/Thracian language in understandings of Bithynian identity.

We thus have very little indication of what it meant to be Bithynian to Bithynians, or whether this identity was even contrasted with Greek identity in the kingdom, as is so often assumed.[160] It is worth nothing that under the Romans, the region's provincial *koinon* identified itself as consisting of the "Hellenes in Bithynia."[161] One can even imagine that the Bithynian kings, intentionally or not, effected the blurring of ethnic lines through an ambiguity between ethnic and political meanings of 'Bithynian,' the latter referring simply to subjects of the crown. That writers like Strabo still insisted on this distinction could reflect their prioritization of earlier ethnographic categories, or the fraught relationship that imperial writers had with Roman power.

---

158 For a discussion of all these local historians, see M. Dana 2016, 171–240.
159 Fernoux 2004, 73–93; Corsten 2007; D. Dana 2016. Corsten in particular notes that it is at least possible that such names also indicate Thracian mercenaries. To this I would add the possibility that, in a kingdom where most of the rulers bore 'non-Greek' names, even Greeks may have come to adopt 'Thraco-Bithynian' names, though they may not have emphasized the difference as much as we do.
160 The existence of a few Thracian-style *tholos* tombs (cf. Mellink 1970, 175–76) hardly suggests a pattern of any significance.
161 Mitchell 2000, 124.

2.6 Galatians

The early Hellenistic migration of Celtic-speaking peoples into central Anatolia (predominantly northern Phrygia), referred to in our sources as Galatians, is somewhat well-known. Less widespread is an understanding of the ethnic unity, or lack thereof, of these peoples, despite the importance recent works by Mitchell and Strobel. The key ancient text is Strabo, who describes a federated 'tribal' structure consisting of three *ethnê* – the Trokmoi, Tolistobogioi, and Tektosages – which were in turn divided into four tetrachies that supplied tetrarchs, judges, military commanders, and councilors for the entire Galatian community (12.1.5). Based on this passage alongside comparative study of other ancient Celtic societies, Strobel argues that the 'Galatians' were originally ethnically distinct groups that, starting in the late third century, underwent a process of ethnogenesis that was cemented first by a brief period of monarchic rule in the wake of the Mithridatic wars, and subsequently by a *koinon* of the Galatians under direct Roman rule.[162] Both Strabo and archaeological study of the regions settled by the Galatians indicate shared language and material culture across the three *ethnê* that may have contributed to the process of ethnic unification. The political factors behind this process have yet to be investigated, the subject of Strobel's promised second volume in his study of the Galatians.[163] At the same time, the Galatians adopted or supported many of the older cults in the region; whether this led to a merging of identities between the pre-existing population and the Galatian migrants, as Strobel insists, remains unclear.[164] The argument depends on associating material culture with identity, which as we have seen itself requires an emic assertion of such a connection that is lacking in our written evidence.

2.7 Phrygians?

The question mark in this section's title indicates my aim to challenge the existence of the Phrygians as a self-conscious people. This may come as a surprise, since they represent one of the better-known inhabitants of ancient Anatolia, thanks especially to the legends surrounding Midas in Greco-Roman literature. Yet it is also common knowledge that internal evidence for what 'Phrygians' called themselves has not survived. They certainly did not call themselves

---

162   Strobel 2002; 2009, 122–28; cf. Strobel 1996. On the Galatian *koinon*, see Mitchell 2000, 123–24. Mitchell (1993, 27–29) argues that the institutions described by Strabo only developed in the second century.
163   Strobel 1996, 271; see also 139–42 on the linguistic unity of the region.
164   Strobel 2009, 124–25.

Phrygians (Gr. *Phruges*), as their language lacks aspirated consonants.[165] The name Phrygian comes from Greek sources, most fundamentally Homer, who mentions them as allies of the Trojans several times and seems to locate them primarily in what was to become Bithynia. They inhabit a land of wealth, but we do not learn much else.[166] Herodotos is not particularly helpful either: he provides no Phrygian *logos* and only explains (during his Egyptian *logos*) that the Phrygians were the oldest people in existence (2.2); later he relates the Macedonian story that the Phrygians once lived in the Balkans as "Briges" before migrating to Asia (7.73). We will return to the second comment below, when discussing origins. While scholars are rightly skeptical of the details of these and subsequent reports on Phrygians in our Greek sources, they do not question the coherence of the Phrygian ethnic group itself as represented by these same sources.[167] Yet it has been shown that such reports have at best a tenuous connection with Phrygia itself, usually only indirectly through encounters with slaves.[168]

The primary basis for seeing the Phrygians as a people is the existence of a powerful kingdom based at Gordion in the Early Iron Age, confirmed by excavation as well as contemporary Assyrian texts, and as Phrygian-speaking by inscriptions clustered in the river valleys dominated by Gordion and in the highland regions to the west, all of which are then connected to the Greek evidence.[169] Not only the script but also forms of monumental architecture associated with political, religious, and funerary contexts seem to have emanated from the dynasty at Gordion and influenced a relatively uniform elite culture.[170] That this culture had a name for itself is possible, but two challenges are, first, determining whether we can equate political control with the presence of material culture (we probably cannot) and, second, knowing what this name was.[171] Besides the fact that 'Phrygian' was a Greek term, there is the

---

165   Brixhe 2007, 149–50. It is unlikely that they called themselves *Bruges*, as Brixhe suggests, since Greeks were perfectly capable of pronouncing this term. See below for further discussion of how these terms relate to Phrygian origins.
166   *Iliad* 2.862–63, 13.793, 18.290–92, 24.544–46.
167   An exception is Laminger-Pascher (1989, 17–40), who posits the conflation of many peoples, including the Mysians, under the name 'Phrygian' in our Greek sources.
168   Rivas 2005; Andreeva 2020.
169   Kingdom: Barnett 1967; Voigt and Henrickson 2000; Voigt 2011; Muscarella 2013 (= 1995); Roller 2011; Summers 2013; Tanaka 2018, 64–68. For a more skeptical view of Phrygia as a centralized state, see Genz 2011, 360–61. Language: Diakonoff and Neroznak 1985; Brixhe 1984, 2004, 2007, 2012, 2013.
170   Wittke 2004, 191–289; Berndt-Ersöz 2006, 143–211. Cf. Innocente 1995, 216–19.
171   On the difficulty of equating material culture with political control, see Strobel 2001, 47–49; Roller 2011, 563; van Dongen 2017; Summers 2018, 110.

inconvenience of the Assyrian evidence, which refers to Midas (*Mita*) as king of the Mushku. Efforts to resolve the Greek and Assyrian perspectives have ranged from simply equating the two terms to rejecting the equivalence to hypothesizing that the Mushku were an eastern Anatolian people associated by the Assyrians with areas beyond their control.[172] According to this last view, the Assyrians continued to identify the region with the Mushku even after the Phrygians, based further to the west, conquered them.[173] A possibility that is not considered, but which is just as likely, is that both Greeks and Assyrians had the name wrong, and that a third name was used by the Phrygian rulers and their subjects, which fell out of usage with the collapse of the kingdom and its satellites over the course of the seventh and early sixth centuries. Finally, we cannot discount a fourth option: that the dynasty defined their power only in political terms, without reference to common ethnicity or culture.

The Greek word 'Phrygian' is suspicious on more than just linguistic grounds. The references in Homer along with two Hellenistic sources suggest that the term referred originally to a people living in what was later called Hellespontine Phrygia.[174] Pseudo-Skylax (94) identifies Phrygia as an *ethnos* in connection with the Hellespontine and Bithynian *poleis* Myrleia, Kyzikos, Priapos, Lampsakos, and Abydos. Moreover, a third-century inscription from Zeleia (*SIG*³ 279) refers to a group of non-citizens who lived in villages within Zeleian territory as *Phruges*. Two highly fragmentary and understudied inscriptions, possibly of early Roman date, also reveal a community that identified as "Almourenian Phrygians."[175] These "Phrygians" are clearly much more localized and distinct from 'Greater Phrygia' in central Anatolia. If we can connect the Homeric usage to the Zeleian terminology, then it seems that there may have been Phrygians, identified by and distinguished from at least one coastal city, though it is important to note that even this inscription represents an externally imposed identity.[176] In any case, these were not the Phrygians of ancient ethnographers or modern scholars, who have generalized, consciously

---

172 Equivalence: Barnett 1967; Kopanias 2015. Rejection: Laminger-Pascher 1989, 17–24.
173 Distinct but equated by Assyrians: Wittke 2004, followed by Roller 2011.
174 On the Homeric geography, see Laminger-Pascher 1989, 11–12; Wittke 2004, 208–13 and 226–29. It is true that Homer also connects Phrygians with the Sangarios River, and therefore Gordion, but not more closely than with Hellespontine Askania. Given Homer's Aegean vantage point, it is more likely that he generalized from west to east rather than vice versa.
175 Fontrier 1896: 376 (#2); Keil and Premerstein 1914, 97 (#142).
176 Cf. Corsaro 1984, 473–77.

or not, from the inhabitants of the Hellespont to refer to all peoples between this latter region and Kappadokia by the same name.[177]

For later periods, the central question is what level of continuity existed to sustain whatever identity (if any) had developed under the Phrygian kings. In favor of continuity are the continued occupation of important sites like Gordion, the preservation of the language all the way until Late Antiquity, and the maintenance of important Phrygian cults, especially that of *Matar*, or Kybele, at both Gordion and Midas City.[178] Yet other than language (on which see below), all of this evidence reflects local rather than regionally connected practices.[179] Institutionally, it is unlikely that the Achaemenids sought to sustain a broad regional identity. Our Greek authors claim that Greater Phrygia was a Persian satrapy, but the lack of any *dahyu* designation in the Persian evidence for such a large region as Phrygia seems telling of the lack of ethnic unity at this point.[180] Indeed, Peter Thonemann has argued that from the Persian conquest onward, the inhabitants of Phrygia developed dispersed forms of life that represented a rejection of state institutions and society, which represented Persian, Macedonian, Galatian, or Roman rule.[181] He does not spell out the implications of this for our understanding of Phrygian identity, but to me this suggests that mechanisms for an identity that stretched across hundreds of miles of the central Anatolian plateau – a much larger area than for any other people except for the likewise uncertain Kappadokians – no longer existed. Thonemann's survey makes clear that more local forms of identity were at play in the region, and that this was further encouraged by the city foundations in the Hellenistic and Roman periods, which promoted civic identity. It is also worth noting that Strabo only mentions Phrygians in passing and never elaborates on which communities comprised this ethnic group.[182]

---

177   Cf. Strobel 2001, 43–49, critiquing the conflation of culture and language with Phrygian ethnicity.
178   Generally: Roller 2011 and 2014. Cult: Roller 1991; Bøgh 2007.
179   Cf. Laminger-Pascher 1989, 41–49, arguing that the continuation of "Phrygian" tomb styles reflects the preservation of older Anatolian burial practices to which the Phrygians themselves were indebted.
180   Cf. Summers 2018 on the Persian destruction of the Phrygian colony at Pteria/Derkenes, which seems to have been the last concentrated settlement linked with the old kingdom at Gordion.
181   Thonemann 2013.
182   12.1.3, 12.3.9, 12.4.1 and 4, 12.7.2, 13.4.12, 14.5.22. It is true that Strabo carefully defines Greater Phrygia (12.8.13), but excludes Pessinous, with its important 'Phrygian' Kybele shrine, and includes Macedonian colonies as well as cities like Aphrodisias that understood their past as more entwined with Karians. His avoidance of the term 'Phrygian' here suggests that he is concerned with geography alone in this section. Cf. Laminger-Pascher 1989, 9–14, who

This argument bears on the other key markers of Phrygian identity, language and cult. The preservation of the Phrygian language, if more than just the observance of religious formulae, could easily have been understood in such local terms (rural communal identity in contrast to Greek or Latin-speaking cities) without linking local linguistic practice to similar speech across the region.[183] Likewise, the continued importance of the Great Mother cult was not distinctive to Phrygia (as we have seen especially in Lydia) and only referred to as "Phrygian" outside of Phrygia itself.[184] Meanwhile, the old sites at Gordion and Midas City became profoundly local in scope, housing small or domestic shrines to the goddess.[185] Indeed, the most important Kybele sanctuary in the Hellenistic and Roman periods was at Pessinous, which had no clear connection to the Phrygian kingdom, came to be dominated by Galatian elites by the second century BCE, if not earlier, and was excluded from Phrygia by Strabo (12.8.13). This cult was certainly perceived as 'Phrygian' by other Greeks and Roman writers, but what the inhabitants of Phrygia thought remains unknown.

There was, however, an important development in the Roman period, which coincided with the similar articulation of regional ethnic identity in Lydia discussed above. An explicitly Phrygian institution developed in the form of a Phrygian *koinon* based at Apameia, Laodikeia began representing a personified Phrygia on its coinage, and hero cults for Homeric Phrygians and Midas emerged in the region. By the third century CE, the local historian Metrophanes had composed a *Phrygiaka* (*FGrH* 796). Kelp questions the linking of these developments with the contemporary appearance of Neo-Phrygian language texts; regardless, it is clear that a Phrygian ethnic community took shape under Roman power and no doubt in response to Roman imperial categories, just as in Lydia.[186] It is, however, misleading to portray this as a revival of a dormant ethnic identity; it is rather a process of identity formation or even ethnogenesis, considering that these evocations of a Phrygian past often were expressed by cities that had been founded by Macedonian rulers, and were intimately bound up with Greco-Roman myths about Phrygia that had not played a role

---

 argues for the multi-ethnic nature of Greater Phrygia, which was ignored by our Greek sources. The argument depends, however, on inferring ethnic admixture among various peoples from Strabo's descriptions, a problematic inference that ignores the geographer's reliance on literary sources, as we have already discussed.

183 For the argument that "Neo-Phrygian" texts do not suggest that people continued to speak Phrygian, see Laminger-Pascher 1989, 8–9, 49–53. Cf. Bru 2017, 254–84.
184 Robert 1987, 321–23. Cf. Hutter 2006; Talloen et al. 2006.
185 Roller 1999, 189–98.
186 Kelp 2013, 87–92; 2015, 107–214. Kelp also, less convincingly, argues for the importance of the goddess Kybele as an indicator of Phrygian identity at this time.

in either the Phrygian kingdom or with the inhabitants of Phrygia during the Persian and Hellenistic periods.

2.8 Other Uncertain Peoples

Like the 'Phrygians,' it is questionable whether the remaining 'peoples' of Anatolia mentioned by Herodotos and other writers refer to self-identifying ethnic communities. The labels likely originated outside the regions in question and were only adopted by individuals from these regions in foreign contexts. This observation is not a consensus one, however, so it is worth addressing the evidence for each group in more detail, starting with the Pisidians. This group is not mentioned in our Greek evidence until the fourth century. Herodotos refers to Milyans, Lasonians, Kabalians (possibly another name for Lasonians), and Hytennai in the approximate region of later Pisidia (3.90, 7.77). Yet a few decades later Xenophon mentions Pisidians as a thorn in the Persians' side (e.g., *Anab.* 1.1.11), and few of the Herodotean ethnonyms (e.g., Hytennians) appear here or in later authors. Indeed, the image of the Pisidians as unruly and difficult to subdue becomes a historiographical motif.[187] Meanwhile, scholars link the Milyans variously with Pisidia, Lykia, or both; by the first century BCE they formed a *commune* (*koinon*?) mentioned by Cicero and confirmed by epigraphical evidence.[188] Strabo, drawing on earlier Hellenistic sources, refers also to the Kabalians, connecting them with Homeric Solymoi – ignoring Herodotos, who links the Milyans with the Solymoi – but also with subsequent Lydian and Pisidian migrations (13.4.15–17). Our only emic evidence comes from the city of Termessos, which in the second century CE began advertising Solymean heritage.[189]

This confusing and meagre evidence has led to the conclusion that Pisidia was a region of diverse peoples and languages, although the term Pisidian is still used to refer to a coherent ethnic group.[190] We can identify some of these peoples, such as the Milyadeis (Milyans), but Herodotos' Hytennians and Lasonians remind us that such ethnic identities may have been fluid, evolving in and out of existence. Were the Milyans themselves a static group existing since the fifth century, or a community that evolved in response to the aggression of the Lykian League, adopting a Greek ethnographic category, in the late

---

187 Mitchell 1991b, 119–21; Kosmetatou 1997a, 5–7.
188 A. Hall 1986. Cic. *Verr.* 1.95.
189 Syme 1995, 180–92 (also suggesting admixture with "Lycaonians"); Kosmetatou 1997b; de Hoz 2005–2006; Arroyo-Quirce 2020. Cf. Frei 1993, 87–91.
190 For the diversity of the region, see Hemer 1980, 61–64; cf. Talloen 2015, 13–14. Less cautious is Doni 2009. Evidence for the language of the region is sparse, but Brixhe 2016 argues for greater linguistic unity than Hemer.

Hellenistic period? Likewise, the Solymians are only claimed as ancestors by one 'Pisidian' city, as far as we can tell, and otherwise are seen as ancestral to a broader area only by external sources.

The idea of Pisidian migration would seem to offer a coherent interpretation of the evidence, but ultimately falls victim to excessive trust in Greek and Roman points of view. In addition to Strabo's comments on Kibyra, we know that Oinoanda's early name was "Termessos near Oinoanda," suggesting migration from that 'Pisidian' city. Linguistic analysis of names found in inscriptions from the cities of Olbasa and Balboura also show the strong presence of 'Pisidian' names from areas that are perceived to have formed the original core of Pisidian habitation.[191] Yet this core region itself does not witness any expressions of Pisidian identity – as we just mentioned, Termessos vaunts Solymean identity – and it is doubtful that ancient Balbourans (or others) were aware of the subtle linguistic distinctions between 'Pisidian' and 'Milyan' names that modern scholars have dissected.

Indeed, Pisidian (and Kabalian) identity is only claimed by individuals outside of Pisidia itself.[192] This certainly suggests the absence of a proper Pisidian community, and instead the (compulsory?) adoption of outside categories in foreign contexts. This absence is unsurprising given the political fragmentation of the region, with cities often warring with one another.[193] Yet, as with Lydia and Phrygia, we see the Roman imperial period as encouraging expression of regional ethnicity, although in this case in an unexpected area. Kibyra, never associated with the region of Pisidia by ancient authors, begins representing a *Thea Pisidikê* on its coinage, while epitaphs from the plain north of the city invoke the protection of Pisidian gods (*theoi Pisidikoi*).[194] It is true that Strabo identifies Pisidian as one of the four languages of Kibyra, but why such gods only appear here and not in the more traditional region of Pisidia, and what this means for our understanding of Pisidian identity, requires further study. The suggestion that it was important to stress the Pisidian nature of these gods in a borderlands region where other ethnic traditions were present depends on a pre-existing strong sense of Pisidian identity for which, as we have seen, there is no evidence.[195]

The nearby Pamphylians are even less likely to have been an ethnic group, despite Herodotos' representation of them as such through common

---

191   Olbasa: Kearsley 1994. Balboura: Hall and Coulton 1990. See also Robert and Robert 1954, 72–79 and 350–61, who posit further Pisidian migration into Tabai and Kidrama.
192   E.g., Launey 1949, 471–76; La'da 2002, E2314–2321.
193   Kosmetatou 1997a.
194   Robert 1962, 212–19; 1997, 128–139; Akıncı Öztürk and Malay 2012.
195   For this suggestion, see Mitchell 2000, 128.

descent from a Trojan migration led by Amphilochos and Kalchas (7.91; cf. Strabo 14.4.3). The name Pamphylia ("land of mingled tribes"; cf. *LSJ* s.v. πάμφυλος) itself alludes to diversity, an impression reinforced by the political autonomy of the region's cities and the linguistic evidence, which indicates bilingualism involving a local Greek dialect in interaction with the Greek mainland, Cyprus, and non-Greek Anatolians, alongside local non-Greek languages delineated in terms of cities, such as Sidetic.[196] Even later ethnographers do not seem to treat the region's inhabitants as a single ethnic group, nor do individuals abroad label themselves as Pamphylians. On the other hand, a couple Roman-era inscriptions from Termessos refer to a Pamphylian *ethnos*, though the implications of this evidence on questions of ethnicity have yet to be explored.[197]

Another region of uncertain ethnicity is Lykaonia, which is ignored by or unknown to Herodotos. Hieroglyphic Luwian inscriptions from the early first millennium BCE have revealed the presence of a powerful kingdom based in the Konya plain, but give little indication of how anyone in the region saw themselves ethnically.[198] Xenophon indicates that the inhabitants represented a military and administrative unit in the Persian Empire (*Cyr.* 6.2.10; cf. *Anab.* 7.8.25) but otherwise sources refer to the region without any ethnographic discussion (e.g., Strabo 12.6.1–5).[199] We can distinguish 'native' personal and place names in the region, though without knowing what broader identity/-ies to attach to them.[200] A few individuals called "Lykaonians" do show up on epitaphs on Rhodes, but this may reflect Rhodian categories of identity imposed on foreigners whose self-proclaimed origins were too unfamiliar.[201]

To the east of Lykaonia lay the sprawling highland region of Kappadokia, which stretched from Kilikia in the south to the Black Sea, including the region commonly referred to as Pontos by scholars. As with Lykaonia, the Hieroglyphic Luwian inscriptions from the region (especially the kingdom of Tabal) in the early first millennium BCE focus on dynastic identity and place-names, but provide few ethnic identifiers.[202] Herodotos reveals that the Greeks called the inhabitants of this land "Syrians" (1.72; cf. 3.90, 5.49.6, 7.72), a claim that may derive from West Asian imperial discourse, since a Luwian inscription

---

196 Political autonomy: Grainger 2009, 12–56. Pamphylian dialect: Brixhe 1976, esp. 145–50; Brixhe and Tekoğlu 2000. Sidetic: Nollé 1983; Woudhuizen 1984–85.
197 İplikçioğlu, Çelgin, and Çelgin 2007, nos. 13 and 17.
198 Goedegebuure et al. 2020; Massa et al. 2020.
199 Cf. Bellucci 2000, 245.
200 Alkan 2014.
201 Boyxen 2018, 372–73.
202 Hawkins 2000, 424–532.

from Karkamish (A6) refers to the *Sura* next to the Phrygians (*Mushka*) in listing foreign lands. Herodotos' account is followed by subsequent authors, some of whom qualify them as "White Syrians" (*Leukosuroi*).[203] Herodotos also tells us that the term "Kappadokian" is Persian, which aligns with the Achaemenid term for the region, *Katpatuka*. Meanwhile, it seems that the Greek term derived not from the conflation of the inhabitants of Kappadokia with those from the Levant, but rather from the Urartian and Syrian term for Kappadokia, while the prefix *Leuko-* may refer to Hittite word for the *Lukka* peoples or to the river Lykastos in the region.[204] Regardless of which interpretation we prefer, it seems almost certain that both terms represent external perspectives.[205]

The likelihood that there was no self-identifying Kappadokian (or Suran) ethnic group grows when we consider Strabo's testimony. The geographer fails to provide any proper ethnography or origin story for Kappadokians, instead focusing on landscape and administrative information.[206] He does refer to language as a defining feature of this group, but also marks the Kataonians as ethnically distinct (12.1.1–2), suggesting that linguistic unity was an externally perceived trait, and later implies that the sanctuary to Ma-Enyo at Komana was mostly significant for Kataonians (12.2.3).[207] The one exception to this picture of an ethnically diverse region is the sanctuary of Kataonian Apollo, which Strabo claims inspired satellite sanctuaries to be built in other parts of Kappadokia (12.2.6). Unfortunately, little work has been done to better understand this cult and its role in fostering a common identity.

Of course, Kappadokia was ruled by two local dynasties in the Hellenistic period: the southern portion by the Ariarathids and the northern by the Mithridatic dynasty. But in both cases, these rulers vaunted their ancestral ties to the Achaemenid nobility, and many of their elite supporters seem to have likewise been Iranian, if we can judge by the names that come down to us.[208] These names do not guarantee that the dynasties and their nobles exclusively identified as Iranian (or at all), and Strabo suggests that there was an ethnic organization in the Ariarathid kingdom that bound all Kappadokians together, when referring to the Roman alliance with both king and *ethnos* after Apameia

---

203 See Franck 1966 for references.
204 Rollinger 2006; Dan 2010; cf. Leonhard 1915, 291–92. See, however, Simon 2012, who argues that *Sura* was the indigenous name for Kappadokians based on its usage in hieroglyphic Luwian inscriptions.
205 Summerer 2005, 129–35, 151.
206 Panichi 2005.
207 Cf. Bellucci 2000, 243–44.
208 Ballesteros Pastor 2013, 187; McGing 2014; Gatzke 2019; cf Ballesteros Pastor 2006, 390–91 and 2020.

(12.2.11).[209] Yet what institutions lay behind this *ethnos*, whether Iranians were excluded, and what relationship most 'Kappadokians' had to the institutional *ethnos* all remain unanswered questions that future studies might hopefully elucidate. The Roman establishment of a Kappadokian *koinon* in later periods does not seem to have had much impact on ethnic solidarity.[210]

By contrast, Pontic Kappadokia (or simply Pontos) seems to have only been 'Kappadokian' or 'Syrian' in the minds of Greek authors. The Pontic rulers are never credited with fostering any kind of regional ethnic unity, and their support of 'Anatolian' sanctuaries reflected royal relations with local communities. Even Pontic identity was not central to their ideological program, since the term 'Pontic' emanated from cities only during Roman rule and, at times, outside of the province of Pontus in other parts of the Black Sea coast.[211]

To the west of Pontic Kappadokia, the Paphlagonians and Mariandynians are just as poorly understood. Herodotos merely mentions them and describes their similar military equipment (3.90; 7.72). Both groups are conceived by subsequent Greek writers as coming from Thrace and living in the mountainous regions of the northern peninsula west of the Halys River and east of Bithynia.[212] Strabo carefully defines the geographical limits of both regions, but his ethnographic comments are limited to the foundation of shrines on Mount Olgassys by the Paphlagonians, and an admitted confusion about who the Mariandynians were, other than "helots" of the Herakleians (12.3.4, 9, 12, 40).[213] We also know that Paphlagonia was divided into small valley kingdoms until its conquest by the Pontic kings.[214] Some of these dynasts did claim descent from the Homeric Pylaimenes, leader of the Paphlagonian contingent, but to what extent this impacted the self-perception of non-royals in the region remains unknown.[215]

The Mariandynians, by contrast, as a servile population within the territory of Herakleia Pontikê, may have existed as an ethnic group who self-identified in opposition to their oppressors, although Herodotos seems to locate them within a much larger geographical space than the fifth-century territory of the city (3.90). This image seems confirmed by the Herakleian dedication at

---

209 Cf. Gabelko 2017, 324–25.
210 Mitchell 2000, 125.
211 Mitchell 2002; Vitale 2014.
212 Paphlagonians: Leonhard 1915, 300–307. Mariandynians: Strabo 12.3.4.
213 Cf. Paradiso 2007.
214 Barat 2013, 157–65.
215 Mitchell 2010, 92–97. In the same vein, the Athenian stereotypes that Aristophanes plays on in the *Knights* by associating Kleon with a Paphlagonian are unlikely to have influenced communities in Paphlagonia itself.

Olympia, observed by Pausanias, which celebrated a victory over Mariandynian raiders (5.1.26).[216] Strabo locates the act of enslavement during the foundation of Herakleia, but the testimony from Herodotos and Pausanias has led most scholars to posit a more gradual process occurring over the course of the fifth century.[217] The challenge here is that our information about such a group, including the existence of an eponymous ancestor, Mariandynos, all comes from external sources, and possibly even described a situation that once existed but had petered out either due to fourth-century political reform or more gradual territorial shrinkage in the Hellenistic period.[218] Linguistic and archaeological evidence has thus far failed to identify a distinct Mariandynian culture, for example in the recent survey of the non-Greek names of Herakleia.[219]

We end our overview of the uncertain peoples of Anatolia with Kilikia, a region that can be said to have belonged equally to the peninsula and to the Levant. It is commonly divided between the mountainous western half, Rough Kilikia, and Smooth Kilikia, a fertile zone that communicates most easily with the sea and Syria.[220] Despite this geographical partition, Herodotos assigns ethnic unity to the whole, and links Kilikian origins both to Greece, since they were once called *Hypachaioi*, and to the Levant, as Kilix was the son of Phoenician Agenor (7.91; cf. 3.90, 5.49, 7.77; Apollodoros 3.1.2). Strabo hints at this origin story and occasionally speaks of Kilikians as political actors, but otherwise focuses on the individual histories of the region's cities (15.5.1–21), or refers to more locally defined ethnic groups, such as the Homonadensians of northern Rough Kilikia (14.5.1, 24 cf. Pliny *N.H.* 5.94).[221]

The name Kilikia itself likely derives from the Assyrian term for one of the kingdoms in the region, Khilakku.[222] The later Greek tendency to refer to the entire region by one name contrasts with the political and even cultural fragmentation from the Late Bronze Age through the Early Iron Age, when Assyrian, Babylonian, but most importantly Hieroglyphic Luwian sources attest to multiple kingdoms within 'Kilikia,' including not only Khilakku but

---

216 The attempt to link this victory with the reduction of Mariandynians to servile status is rather tentative (on which see Baralis 2015, 208–09), since the Herakleians celebrated a defensive victory rather than an act of conquest.
217 Burstein 1976, 6–11, 28–30, and 58–60; Baralis 2015, 205–09. For a general discussion of the sources, see Paradiso 2007; Baralis 2015, 198–202.
218 Baralis 2015, 217–20; Avram 1984, 22–27.
219 Avram 2013, esp. 62.
220 Casabonne 2004, 21–49.
221 Syme 1995, 219–23. Another example is the Katennians (Strabo 12.7.1).
222 Jasink & Bombardieri 2013, 19–21; cf. Casabonne 2004, 64–67, who also suggests that the kingdom in Smooth Kilikia, Que, may have been an Assyrian abbreviation for Luwian *Kuwa-liga* (but see next note).

also Que, possibly a distortion of the local Luwian name, Hiyawa.[223] It was only with the Achaemenids that Kilikia became a unified satrapy, ruled by a local dynast, which may have influenced the ethnographic category used by Herodotos and later writers.[224] Yet after Alexander the region again became divided between the Ptolemaic and Seleukid empires until the early second century.[225] With the decline of these powers, Rough Kilikia seems to have become home to local potentates, branded as pirates and marauders by our hostile literary sources, while Smooth Kilikia eventually became divided between the Romans, who sought to foster self-administrating cities on the coast, and local client-kings.[226] Between the fall of the Achaemenids and the creation of an inclusive Kilikian province under Vespasian, there was, therefore, little institutional foundation for the development of a common Kilikian identity in the region, nor were there any cults or local organizations shared by all of its inhabitants.[227] The urbanization of the coast, by contrast, seems to have encouraged the emergence of distinct local identities.[228]

Linguistic and onomastic evidence reveals a strong Luwian linguistic element throughout the region, often referred to as a "substratum."[229] Yet it is also clear that already in the Early Iron Age, Kilikia was multilingual, with significant knowledge of Phoenician and Aramaic among the literate populations.[230] Determining how this linguistic situation related to ethnic identity is difficult, particularly because the textual evidence either employs family or political labels or refers to peoples who do not easily correspond to later populations. An example comes from the two famous Luwian-Phoenician bilingual inscriptions from the eighth century BCE, found at Karatepe and Çineköy, in which local rulers define their power as over Hiyawa and Danunians, and in relation to the house of Mopsos.[231] We will return to this evidence when discussing Kilikian origins and Hellenization, but for now it suffices to point out that the Hiyawa/Danunians were not encouraged to identify together with other Luwian speakers by their king, nor did they persist as a visible ethnic group in subsequent centuries, perhaps effaced by the Achaemenids if not by earlier

---

223 Jasink & Bombardieri 2013. For the evidence, see Hawkins 2000, 38–71. On the possible equivalence of Que and Hiyawa, see Bryce 2016, 74.
224 Casabonne 2001 and 2004, 165–85. Cf. Meyer 2004, 11–12.
225 Tempesta 2013; Sayar 2004, 17–20; Meyer 2001.
226 Desideri 2001, 141–43; Tobin 2001; Trampedach 2011.
227 Elton 2007.
228 Meyer 2001; Sayar 2004, 21–28.
229 Houwink ten Cate 1965; Casabonne 2004, 59–73; Payne 2006, 120–25.
230 Yakubovitch 2015 even argues that Phoenician was the official language of the kings of Adana/Hiyawa, which he equates with the Que of Assyrian texts.
231 Karatepe: *KAI* 26. Younger 1998. Çineköy: Tekoğlu et al. 2000.

political developments. The Persians themselves, whatever political unity they promoted, fostered linguistic diversity through the adoption of Aramaic as an official language.[232]

With local and especially civic identity predominant in Kilikia itself, we must look abroad to find self-identifying Kilikians. Even here instances are incredibly rare, with the important exception of Ptolemaic Cyprus and Egypt, where a *koinon* and a *politeuma* of Kilikians, respectively, are attested.[233] In these particular contexts, and likely encouraged by Ptolemaic military and administrative categories, small Kilikian ethnic communities emerged. Elsewhere, including in Kilikia itself, this is unlikely. Even where specific communities adopted or instigated origin myths involving settlement by Amphilochos, Kalchas, or Mopsos, this was never articulated to foster commonality with other Kilikian cities, but with more distant communities in Pamphylia and western Asia Minor.[234]

2.9 Anatolians?

Before concluding this section, it is worth considering to what extent the various peoples (and smaller communities, where regional ethnic groups are uncertain) shared a broader culture that might be termed 'Anatolian.' This adjective, when it is not used as in the above discussion simply as a geographical designation for diverse and distinct groups, plays an important role in transregional or comparative studies of the peninsula, typically indicating commonality either through opposition to non-Anatolian groups like Greeks, Persians, or Romans, or with respect to characteristics shared across several regions (or both). In the former usage, Anatolian becomes a blanket term for 'indigenous' peoples or culture, as for example in Louis Robert's foundational onomastic study, *Noms indigènes dans l'Asie Mineure gréco-romaine*, which sought to "rescue" Greek names from being misidentified as indigenous, but without further interrogating the truly indigenous names, as he saw them, in terms of their own linguistic differences.[235]

More recently, a few studies have emerged that claim to be about Anatolia. Stephen Mitchell defines the region culturally by its interior peoples, as distinct from the coastal west, and identifies three main Anatolian zones in which he observes cultural commonality: the interior (Mysians, Lydians, and Phrygians),

---

232 Casabonne 2004, 93–97.
233 Tempesta 2013, 36–38; Launey 1949, 476–81.
234 Scheer 1993, 153–305.
235 Robert 1963. For the critique, see Brixhe 2013, 22–24.

the Pontic north, and the Taurus mountain range to the south.[236] Christian Marek, whose study of Asia Minor delineates the region geographically without a commitment to cultural unity, nevertheless employs the adjectives "Anatolian" and "indigenous" in ways that suggest regional similarities among local peoples and early migrants like Phrygians and Hittites, who are distinct from immigrants and outsiders such as "Romans, Celts, Jews, Macedonians, Iranians, Greeks, Aramaeans, and Assyrians."[237] Lucia Novakova more explicitly claims to explore Anatolian identity, but limits her investigations to Karians and Lykians, along with more implicit consideration of Lydians, Phrygians, and Mysians.[238] There is overlap among these studies, but also significant areas of difference and contradiction.

There is also the tendency to refer to Anatolian (or indigenous) culture when a particular practice, object, or form can be found in multiple regions. Worship of deities like the Great Mother, Men, or a fatherly storm god – with various names in Anatolian languages and Greek – is an obvious example that appeared in our discussion of Lydian and Phrygian religious traditions. Another example in the realm of religion comes from confessional rites during the Roman period. Beyond cult, one observes tumuli, rock-cut tombs, monumental architecture and sculpture, or pottery style across several regions.[239] In one sense, all of these things are 'Anatolian' because they occurred in Anatolia, sometimes even exclusively. On the other hand, nothing occurs everywhere in the region, and much in this selective list shows up beyond the peninsula, whether in the Greek world, Thrace, or other parts of Southwest Asia. More importantly, there is nothing to indicate that such transregional commonalities were perceived as important linkages between ethnic or communal groups. Thus, while we can speak coherently about Anatolian culture when looking at a particular assemblage, not only does this coherence disappear when multiple assemblages are considered together – worship of Kybele does not, for example, map precisely onto areas where rock-cut tombs are built – but the very desire for such coherence is revealed as explicitly modern, and at times nationalistic, since that coherence seems not to have mattered in antiquity.[240]

The use of 'Anatolian' to exclude Greeks and Greek culture is also problematic, largely because dozens of 'Greek' communities, especially on the western

---

236 Mitchell 1993, 5–7, 170–76, 187–95, and 2017.
237 Marek 2016, 1, 3, 397–400.
238 Novakova 2019, esp. 194–204 (= Novakova 2017).
239 Burial evidence: Novakova 2019, 79–99, 120–39. Monuments: Işık 2009, 2010, 2016.
240 For an interpretation driven by nationalistic motives, see Işık 2016 for the notion of an Anatolian-Ionian "essence" (with 'Ionian' understood as purely Anatolian) that defines this ancient essence in implicit relation to the modern boundaries of Turkey.

seaboard, developed contemporarily with the non-Greek peoples and communities in the rest of the peninsula. Indeed, their Greek identity emerged centuries after settlement. In other words, their communal histories in Anatolia coincide with the communal histories of Lydians, Karians, and others, making it difficult to know why these Ionians, Aiolians, and Dorians are less Anatolian than their neighbors.[241] I lack the space to fully explore this question, but the centrality of local identity, cults, and even material culture to these communities clearly outweighs the linguistic, political, and cultural ties to mainland Greece. The point is not that these cities were more Anatolian than Greek, but that they demonstrate the uselessness of such a binary opposition.

2.10 *Summary*

This section has labored to illuminate the challenges involved in defining who the people of Anatolia were, in order to call into question the salience, and in many cases the reality, of the regional ethnic identities described by outside observers like Herodotos, Strabo, and most modern scholars. As with so much in the field of ancient history, many of these challenges stem from problems with the evidence. Any attempt to properly understand the peoples of Anatolia must reckon with the dueling consciousness within every text that has sought to describe one or more ethnic communities in the region, from ancient histories and geographic treatises to modern scholarship. The desire to accurately represent these communities is tempered and informed by the aim to have these representations make sense to the presumed reader. What "makes sense," of course, comes down not only to what is semantically comprehensible, but also to what conforms to this reader's worldview and expectations. For Anatolia, our knowledge stems largely from the imperial gaze of Hittite, Assyrian, Persian, Macedonian, and Roman rulers, along with 'Greek' writers a few Latin texts. In all of these cases, both the content of knowledge about the inhabitants of Anatolia and the very terms used to label these inhabitants were shaped and influenced by externally imposed categories of organization, such as the *dahyava* of the Achaemenids, Greek *ethnê* (or *genê*), Roman *gentes* and *provinciae*, or the modern nation-state, as much if not more than by the self-perceptions of the inhabitants themselves.

Recognition of the fundamentally etic nature of our evidence is at best piecemeal in modern scholarship; indeed, my choice to start each subsection with Herodotos was meant to mirror (and then problematize) the general tendency to start with what the Greeks say. The result of this tendency is that the existence of most of the peoples of Anatolia is taken for granted rather than

---

241 Cf. Crielaard 2009; Greaves 2019.

viewed as a question in need of answering. Likewise, the importance of 'peoplehood' itself, i.e., ethnic identity, to the inhabitants of Anatolia is assumed. It is hard not to see such willingness to follow ancient ethnographers (and imperial rulers) as due at least in part to the alluring parallelism between their ethnic categories and the modern nation-state.[242]

A research perspective is not the place to overturn such tendencies, but I do hope to have convinced future scholars to reconsider them, and to have suggested paths forward for the several regions discussed. One broader starting point is to stop avoiding or superficially utilizing theories of identity and ethnicity that have become central to studies of the Greeks and other groups outside Anatolia; as we have seen, this habit is all too common in studies of the peoples of Anatolia.[243] While such studies generally agree that identity, and ethnic identity by consequence, is something self-perceived and articulated, and therefore socially constructed, dynamic and fluid rather than static or fixed, they do not in practice discuss ethnic communities according to these criteria. Established theory commits the investigator of a particular people to first of all look for emic articulations of a common identity, then to link these articulations to shared traits and to the social meanings and institutions that make them possible. It also insists on taking notice of changes to these articulations without taking for granted that such identities had an existence independent of them.

In contrast to such a theoretically guided approach to ethnic groups, work on Anatolian peoples has generally assumed that if an outside group or person, e.g., Herodotos, tells us a people existed, then it must have done so, regardless of whether and how often individuals supposedly from this people expressed themselves in such terms. One then assumes a fixed existence across time of this people, though at times admitting to changes in what it meant to be that people, and focuses on using archaeology and linguistic evidence to link peoples to 'culture,' i.e., to grouped objects, etc. that appear similar from a vantage point – the hindsight of two millennia later – that no ancient inhabitant of Anatolia could hope to have shared.

This under-theorization in studies of Anatolian peoples does not invalidate the work I have discussed, as I hope this section has shown. Important data has been marshalled and crucial questions raised, but all too often easy, albeit elaborate, answers are reached due to faulty assumptions and circular reasoning. Key topics are made of peoples who may not have existed except in the minds of foreign writers and powers, or who existed as peoples in a secondary

---

242   For the role of nationalism in studies of ancient ethnicity, see Ruby 2006, 28–37.
243   A notable, if regrettably underutilized, exception is Strobel 2001.

way in relation to smaller communities, communities that were able to lay claim to the allegiance of individuals in much more impactful ways politically and socially – let us not forget that Herodotos himself tells us that he was a Halikarnassian, not a Greek, Dorian, or Karian, in his preface. The upside is that there is great opportunity for future work that brings a more theoretically grounded approach to these topics. It is my hope that the critiques in this work will encourage studies that both dispense with unwarranted assumptions and make their chief methodological principle to begin with the evidence of a 'people's' own views on the matter, not only in order to define what made up a particular ethnic identity, but to determine whether and to what extent such an identity mattered at all.

3 Origins

The consequences of applying a simplistic, usually unstated, understanding of ethnicity shows up most acutely in scholarly discussions of the origins of the main peoples of Anatolia, with the exception of the Galatians, whose geographic origins and process of ethnogenesis have already been discussed. In particular, the assumption that ethnic groups are fixed entities, whose existence, once established for a particular moment, can be taken for granted across time and even space, dominates such discussions. Thus, not only is the literary evidence from later periods used to establish the existence of peoples in often uncritical fashion, as I affirmed in the last section, but this questionable conclusion is then used to retroject that existence back into the prehistoric past, connecting first-millennium peoples to evidence from the Bronze Age. If a group like the Phrygians had no antecedent in the second-millennium Anatolian landscape, then it must have come from somewhere, and the task becomes locating a land of emigration. The notion of ethnogenesis as a process of identity construction in specific social and political circumstances remains absent.

In pursuing questions of origins in such a fashion, scholars model the habit of calling Myceneans "Greek," for the logic that informs this constructed link is the same. First, they look for the presence of names for places and polities in (especially) the Hittite imperial texts that 'resemble' later place names in the first millennium. Just as pre-modern Aegeanists connect Hittite Ahhiya(wa) to the Mycenean world, although now with some nuance, so those investigating the origins of the peoples of Anatolia seek to draw equivalence between states and regions like the Lukka lands and Mira, on the one hand, and Lykians and

Lydians, on the other.[244] The problem of whether the Hittite terms represented how the peoples inhabiting these lands understood themselves is never seriously broached.

A second basis for linking Bronze Age evidence to the populations of Iron Age Anatolia is historical linguistics, which more famously helped to establish the Myceneans as 'Greeks' when it was revealed that they wrote an early form of Greek. As we saw in the preceding section, the centrality of language to ethnic identity serves as an article of faith for many scholars, despite its secondary – i.e., neither necessary nor sufficient – role in theories of ethnicity. This allows these scholars to trace earlier evolutions of and kinship among the various Anatolian languages (or lack thereof) to supposed population movements, leading to interesting but, as I will argue, problematic theories of migration during or after the Bronze Age to help explain discrepancies between the Hittite evidence and the ethnic map from the following millennium. The fact that language can enter a geographical space without the migration of an entire population seems too inconvenient for such arguments to consider.

Finally, material cultural assemblages, e.g., of ceramics, are identified and at times linked to the Hittite place names and Anatolian linguistic groups. This practice is less common and has not gone unchallenged. Mac Sweeney has, for instance, argued against inferring ethnic identity from the material evidence in favor of a more locally inscribed communal identity, and Pavúk points out that ceramic cultures rarely correspond to Hittite political geography.[245] Yet such critiques have not swayed everyone.

Before more fully assessing the arguments in favor of connecting the peoples of Anatolia to Bronze Age origins, it will be helpful to establish this Hittite political geography more precisely. Of course, Hatti itself dominated central eastern Anatolia, a land equivalent to parts of later Kappadokia. To the north were the Kaska (or Gasga), in the mountainous regions of later Pontic Kappadokia, and the Pala in later Paphlagonia. To the south was Kizzuwatna (Smooth Kilikia) and Tarhuntassa (Rough Kilikia and possibly Pamphylia). Further west, specific locations of place names are contested, debates to which we will return as they are relevant to discussions of origins. Here, it will suffice to simply name those most pertinent to this discussion: Pedassa, the Lukka, the Karkisa, Masa, the kingdom of Arzawa, which consisted of the smaller regions of Mira, Kuwaliya, the Seha River Land, Appawiya and Hapalla, and

---

244   E.g., Forlanini 2013. As an example of similar studies of the Mycenean world, see, e.g., Kopanias 2021.
245   Mac Sweeney 2011; Pavúk 2015.

finally Wilusa.[246] Scholars have more difficulty locating another important group mentioned in the Hittite records, the Luwiya; the two leading candidates are southeastern Anatolia and the west of the peninsula, related to but not equivalent to the later kingdom of Arzawa.[247] Let us now turn to the origins of specific peoples, following the same order as in the preceding section.

The Lydians present a problem for the general methodology articulated above, in that there is no clear Hittite place name that obviously corresponds to their name. However, an improved understanding of the relationship between Lydian and Luwian, the language assumed to have been spoken throughout much of western Anatolia in the Bronze Age, has altered this picture.[248] Previously believed to have been a descendant of Luwian, Lydian is now known to represent a distinct branch within the Anatolian language family tree. Moreover, the root *luw-* in Luwian would be equivalent to the root **lud-* in Lydian, meaning that the Lydian word for *Luwiya* would be *Ludiya*. The problem is, of course, that the Lydians, according to the logic that equates language and people, were not Luwians. Yet this problem is easily solved by supposing that the Lydians migrated from elsewhere, adopting the local name for the region, *Luwiya*, but coming to pronounce it in their own language as *Ludiya* (Greek *Ludia*).[249]

This theory is aided by the fact that, as we have seen, Greek authors, making use of Homer, believed that the Lydians were once called Meionians (later, Maionians). The name change can be imagined to have resulted from their supposed migration into Luwiya/Lydia. In addition, the name Meionian/Maionian can be linked to the Hittite place-name Masa, which would, according to some reconstructions, place them in northwestern Anatolia during the Bronze Age before their supposed migration into historical Lydia.[250] Yet the entire reconstruction has not achieved consensus, with some rejecting the claim that western Anatolia was Luwian-speaking in the Bronze Age.[251] Moreover, such a reconstruction assumes the fixed and static nature of the Meionian/Lydian people and rests on two unprovable assumptions: that the Hittite term Masa reflects a local identity rather than an imposed label, and that the same

---

246 Singer 1983.
247 Melchert 2003, 1–3, 23–26; Bryce 2003, 27–92; Yakubovitch 2010, 239–47.
248 Cf. Yakubovitch 2008. See, however, the doubts about the presence of Luwian in this region by Melchert 2010.
249 Beekes 2003; Widmer 2004; Hönigman and Oettinger 2018, 68–72. See, however, Talamo 1979, 65–98, who argues that this group called themselves Meionians even in Homer's day and only became "Lydians" with Gyges in the seventh century.
250 Beekes 2002, 205–17; Forlanini 2003. Cf. Carruba 2003; Hönigman and Oettinger 2018, 108. See also the discussion below on Phrygian origins for attempts to link Masa to this ethnic group instead.
251 Yakubovitch 2010, 75–157; Oreshko 2013, 89–93; Fontaine 2018. Cf. Roosevelt 2010.

can be said for the Homeric and Greek terms *Meiones* and *Ludoi*.[252] Certainly, the fact that Xanthos refers to Lydians means that by the fifth century 'Lydian' had become internalized by at least some of the region's inhabitants, but because he wrote his work in Greek, this may have only represented an acknowledgement of how to refer to his people in the language and mindset of outsiders. The Lydian language texts, sparse as they are, coupled with the correspondence between *sfardeti* and Persian *Sparda*, speak against 'Lydian' or 'Meionian' as indigenous terms of ethnic identity – although the variant Maionian does seem to have described a district in Lydia that served as an identity marker in later periods.[253]

Once we recognize the external nature of the word Lydian, then the question of origins must be answered in two ways. First, we must determine when the 'Sfardian' community developed, both as an urban and broader ethnic community. The former is tied to the settlement history of Sardis itself, while the latter has thus far been ignored in favor of an assumed transhistorical Lydian community. Second, it would be worthwhile to trace the adoption of the label 'Lydian' by the Lydians themselves. Xanthos represents merely a starting point, but we have yet to investigate to what extent this term was appropriated by Lydians and for what reasons.[254] Both questions are key prerequisites to understanding the origins of the Lydians as a process of socially constructed ethnogenesis.

The question of Mysian origins is even more dependent on the Greek sources, since there is no clear Hittite term, unless one divorces the Lydians from Hittite-named *Masa*, nor any Anatolian language to link them to.[255] As discussed above, there was debate already in antiquity between those who saw the Mysians as Lydian colonists (Herodotos and Xanthos) and those who understood the Mysians as migrants from Thrace (Artemidoros, Strabo, et al.). Neither supposition is particularly credible. The first represents Lydian propaganda to justify their domination of the Mysians under the Mermnads and a presumed feeling of superiority in later periods, while the second is clearly the result of an academic exercise to validate the veracity of Homer, by demonstrating that the *Iliad*'s placing of the Mysians in Thrace was not an error but reflected a migration. Herodotos seems unaware of this theory, meaning that

---

252   Cf. the unpublished argument of Oreshko (located in summaries of two talks, one undated, the other from 2017, at: https://orient-mediterranee.academia.edu/RostislavOreshko/Talks) that the presence of 'non-Anatolian' personal and divine names in the Lydian texts suggests an important Balkan element in Lydian "ethno-linguistic" identity.
253   *TAM* V.1 202, 240; *TAM* V.3 1540; *SEG* 9: 484.
254   My suggestions in the previous section will hopefully serve as a starting point for doing so.
255   For this argument, see Oreshko 2017, 55–59.

it was probably concocted after his lifetime, and Strabo's attempt to buttress it by linking the Mysians with the Moesians is probably just bad linguistics, retrojecting the iotacism of upsilon and *oi* in *koinê* Greek back to a time when such vowel sounds were quite distinct (12.3.3; cf. *Schol. ad Apoll. Rh.* 1.1115).

The alternative is again to trace a process of ethnogenesis during the first millennium, which is still challenging given the lack of evidence. We can, however, plausibly speculate that the Mermnad conquest imposed a shared category (and experience of subjection) that differentiated 'Mysian' peoples from those from *Sfarda*. Such a common experience could have led to the emergence of a shared identity, which would have been strengthened (or developed for the first time) by the experience of rule under and resistance to the Achaemenids. I present this as a scenario to be improved upon, but as imperfect as my reconstruction is, it has the advantage of moving past the faulty assumptions of ancient and modern discussions.

The debate over Karian origins also dates back to antiquity. Herodotos, as we have seen, prefers to see the Karians as migrants from the Aegean islands, while still transmitting the Karian belief that they were *autochthones*. By contrast, he believes that the Kaunians were truly *autochthones*, despite their claim that they had migrated from Krete. The Kretan migration story was extended by later authors to include the Karians and was even adopted in the Hellenistic period by several Karian communities, including Mylasa, Euromos, and Amyzon, as suggested by their worship of a "Kretan-born" Zeus.[256] On the other hand, the Hittite texts mention a *Karkisa* in western Anatolia during the Bronze Age, which is seen as equivalent to first millennium Karians.[257]

Modern attempts to reconcile this evidence has resulted in a coherent picture, albeit one still founded on faulty assumptions. Most view the region as essentially Karian in the Bronze Age, with the truth of the ancient evidence confirmed by the archaeological evidence that reveals Minoan and Mycenean influence and even settlement at Miletos and Iasos. Homer describes Miletos as the main city of the Karians, and later accounts portray Sarpedon as founding the city from Krete, which is taken to reflect a memory of the time before the 'Ionian migration' into the region. Thus, the Karians were both prior inhabitants and early/mid-second millennium migrants.[258]

---

256 Unwin 2017.
257 E.g., Herda 2009, 47–50.
258 Sourvinou-Inwood 2005, 268–309; Unwin 2017, 66–73, 91–123. Cf. Bachvarova 2015, 146–60, who accepts Simon's argument (see subsequent note) but unconvincingly insists on seeing Karkisa as linked to Karians.

As in the case of the Lydians, this argument depends on trusting that the Hittite and Greek sources reflected emic understandings of identity. This trust, however, is not warranted. First, the link between *Karkisa* and later Karians has been undermined on linguistic grounds.[259] In addition, the ascription of a Karian substratum to places like Miletos is problematic because we have no sources from historical Karians that suggest that the city was understood as sharing an ethnic past with them. Kinship ties were often articulated by both Miletos and many Karian communities in the Hellenistic period, but never between each other.[260] Instead, the role of Karians in the Milesian origin stories was to distinguish preexisting inhabitants from incoming groups, even where those current inhabitants were themselves earlier migrants. While such stories linked these inhabitants with actual Karians during the Classical and Hellenistic periods in the minds of Milesians, such usage was not particularly concerned with whether those links existed for Karians of the Late Bronze and Early Iron ages.[261]

It is true that the term Karian was used by Karian communities in fourth-century inscriptions not meant primarily for a broader Greek audience (see above). Yet the context of such usage, communications with Persepolis, is important to acknowledge. Rather than seeing the Karian ethnic group as a naturally occurring entity across time, it is vital to attend to the mechanisms of its creation and maintenance, in this case Achaemenid power and administrative structures. One can imagine Karian-speaking communities developing ethnic commonality earlier, certainly as a means of resistance to Persian power during the 'Ionian' revolt and possibly earlier, even during the zenith of the Lydian Empire. Before this – the late seventh century at the earliest – it is difficult to observe any such mechanism. This of course does not invalidate the possibility that there were migrations into the region from the Aegean and even Krete specifically, but it does indicate that such migrations were not absorbed or resisted by a self-aware Karian people, and that instead the origins of the Karians are to be located in a much later process of ethnogenesis that excluded even some Karian-speaking communities. To speak of Karians (or Greeks) in the region before the seventh century is to mirror the anachronisms of our Greek sources.

---

259 Simon 2011; Oreshko 2019.
260 The exception is the *isopoliteia* agreement between Miletos and Tralles (*Milet* 1.3 143), but the latter city (called Seleukeia in the inscription) was not Karian but Thrakian (Strabo 14.1.42). It is also true that the Milesians claimed kinship with the Kretans, but it is modern logic to calculate an automatic kinship between Milesians and Karians from this.
261 Cf. Mac Sweeney 2015 and 2017 for how such origin stories reflect later (Archaic onward) concerns and perceptions.

The Lykian connection to the *Lukka* lands mentioned in the Hittite texts seems much less controversial, even if there is some debate about the location of these lands in the Bronze Age.[262] Yet the Lykians called themselves *trmmili*, which possibly meant 'mountain-dwelling people,' a name that can be linked to the Hittite place-name *Attarimna*.[263] One suggestion for reconciling these two pieces of evidence is to acknowledge *Attarimna* as the origin of *trmmili* (and *Trmmis*, the Lykian word for the region), and to understand *Lukka* as referring to bands of youths performing preparatory marital rituals in connection with the cult of Apollo.[264] Yet Gander argues that neither Bronze Age term should be associated with later ethnonyms, since *Attarimna* was not even in Lykia, and the Hittite equivalents to later Lykian cities (e.g., *Talawa* > Tlos) were likely not in the Lukka lands either.[265] There are also the stories, from Homer onwards, that suggest a migration from Krete into Lykia, which Bachvarova argues reflects Early Iron Age Anatolian traditions.[266] In the end, the evidence for Lykian origins is actually more confusing than it at first appears, which may explain why many treatments of Lykian identity begin with the Archaic or Classical periods.

One matter of confusion is that there is vagueness around the attempts to connect Hittite place-names to the Lykians. Are scholars simply seeking the origin of the words used to describe the Lykians as a collective, or attempting to locate Bronze Age Lykians? The former is interesting but less relevant to origins, since it can hardly account for why various Lykian-speaking communities chose to call themselves mountainous people. The term *Lukka* is also problematic, since it is quite obvious that the term 'Lykian' was not native until appropriated from Greek-speakers who no doubt were influenced by Hittite terminology, which also (lest we forget) represents an external perspective.[267]

The search for Bronze Age Lykians is even more burdened, since *Attarimna* was a local toponym, not a people, and of course Archaic and Classical

---

262 Bryce (1986, 23–29) situates the Lukka in Karia during the Bronze Age and postulates their migration into Lykia subsequently, while Gander (2016, 80–87) sees the Lukka lands as encompassing SE Lydia, western Lykia, eastern Karia, and parts of Pisidia. Cf. Kolb 2018, 25–44; Oreshko 2020, 18–20.
263 LaRoche 1976; des Courtils 2001; cf. Prost 2007, 104.
264 Eichner 2016.
265 Gander 2016, 80–91.
266 Bachvarova 2015, 146–53, 160–73; cf. Keen 1998, 22–26; Bryce 1986, 29–35.
267 Oreshko 2020, 20–21, insists that *Lukka* is an endonym because there is no evidence to prove that it is an exonym, an argument not only imposing a double standard (since there is precisely no evidence to suggest that it is an endonym), but also ignoring the simple fact that the term's appearance in Hittite texts is itself evidence (however imperfect) that it was an exonym!

inhabitants of the region did not call themselves 'Lykians' except in Greek. As for the Kretan migration tale, it is worth remembering that Herodotos, after taking care to report how Karians and Kaunians understood their own origins, relates Lykian origins without reference to their own beliefs, which suggests that he did not consult Lykians directly. If Homer took inspiration from Anatolian tradition to craft the Bellerophon myth, this would not have prevented him from recasting it in a way that made it relevant to audiences from the Greek mainland as well. But ultimately all of these attempts falter by missing one key point: there are no signs of a regionally coherent ethnic group, or institutions to support this, until the Achaemenid period. Again, ethnic origins, when we relinquish the myth of primordial and static ethnic groups, can be found in later processes of ethnogenesis tied to specific political and social circumstances, in this case subjection to and interaction with the Achaemenid and Athenian empires (see previous section).

With the Bithynians we leave the Hittite evidence altogether, since scholars follow our Greek evidence in seeing this ethnic group as a breakaway group of Thracians who migrated from the Balkan peninsula.[268] To the extent that Paphlagonian (and by implication, Mariandynian) origins are discussed, which is seldom, the same reconstruction applies.[269] This is surprising not only because Greek writers are relatively uninterested in these groups and, by consequence, prone to fitting them into already established categories ('Thracian') and generalizations, but also because the settlement patterns of these regions and, in the case of Paphlagonia, its geography were not conducive to the formation of broader social identities. Dispersed village settlements certainly could evolve regional ties that led to ethnic identity, even in mountainous regions like that of northern Anatolia, but this should not be taken as a given. Instead, the mechanisms and institutions that made possible such identities should be explored as the site of ethnic origins, as Scholten implicitly does in arguing that the Hellenistic rulers of the region "built" Bithynia.[270] We might also imagine that enslavement to the Herakleians led to the construction of the Mariandynian ethnic group. Regarding the Paphlagonians, I have already argued that they were likely not an ethnic group, and thus cannot have an origin as such.

The question of Phrygian origins, which already founders when we question the existence of a self-identifying Phrygian people before the Roman period, is also troubled by the lack of any clear connection with the Hittite evidence.

---

268   E.g., Michels 2009, 12–14.
269   Leonhard 1915, 300.
270   Scholten 2007.

The traditional response to this absence is to follow Herodotos and subsequent ancient authors in claiming that the Phrygians migrated from the Balkans into Anatolia at some point during or after the collapse of Hittite and other centralized powers on the peninsula at the end of the Bronze Age.[271] This despite, and without countering, Drews' withering critique of Herodotos' account as a rationalized invention that contradicted both local Phrygian and earlier Greek beliefs.[272] It is true that linguistic study of Phrygian has revealed close filiation with Thracian and Greek, but languages can spread without mass migration, a possibility strengthened in this case by the dearth of archaeological support for any significant population movement from the Balkans in the period supposed by scholars.[273]

Alternate theories, while generally ignored or less favored, are more persuasive. One option is to suppose migrations of small groups over a long stretch of time, who later became incorporated together through processes of ethnogenesis tied to the formation of the Phrygian kingdom.[274] Another possibility is to associate the Phrygians with the Hittite place-name Masa, based on readings that locate this term in what later became western Phrygia.[275] Finally, there is the least popular theory, that the Phrygians moved westward into central Anatolia during the eighteenth century BCE.[276] But in reality all of these theories speak to the unknown identity espoused (possibly) by what we call the Phrygian kingdom. What is still needed is an account of the ethnogenesis of a self-described 'Phrygian' community, which was likely limited to certain areas near the Hellespont and did not form a regional identity in Greater Phrygia until the Roman period (see above).

For the remaining peoples of Anatolia, the literature on the issue of origins is noticeably miniscule, especially for the Pisidians, Kappadokians, and Lykaonians, perhaps because these groups are simply seen as primordially indigenous. The Lykaonians are unsurprisingly linked with the Bronze Age *Lukka*, and the Kappadokians with the *Sura* mentioned in Urartian and Hieroglyphic Luwian sources or even with the Kaska.[277] Yet it is highly likely, as I have argued above, that none of these terms referred to self-identifying ethnic groups, and if they did, not until the Hellenistic period or later.

---

271   Petrova 1998; Wittke 2004, 229–31; Roller 2011, 560–61.
272   Drews 1993.
273   For the kinship between Phrygian and Thracian and Greek, see Brixhe 2012. On the absence of archaeological traces for a Phrygian migration, see Kopanias 2015.
274   Strobel 2001; Kopanias 2015.
275   Wittke 2004, 185–90; cf. Drews 1993, 17.
276   Drews 1993, 19–26.
277   Lykaonia: E. Laroche 1976, 17. Kappadokians: Barat 2013, 154–56; *Karkamish* A6; see above for further references.

When it comes to Pamphylia and Kilikia, discussions of origins usually revolve around the extent to which these two regions were settled by Greek migrants in the Early Iron Age. The topic thus is intertwined with the question of Hellenization, although in vague fashion because the counterpoint to the Greek settlers is referred to without precision ('indigenous' vel sim.) or by using the external Hittite label 'Luwian,' which was never used by any of the individuals or communities supposed to have been 'Luwian' in the Early Iron Age. In any case, for those who see a significant level of Greek settlement early on, the Pamphylian cities constituted ethnically diverse settlements of Luwians and Greeks even before the Archaic period, with the exception of Archaic foundations like Phaselis.[278] As for Kilikia, the local dynastic texts from the early first millennium make clear that the Luwian term for the kingdom that the Assyrians called Que was *Hiyawa*, which has been controversially connected to the Hittite and Ugaritic term for Myceneans, *Ahhiyawa*. Based on this connection, and the fact that the Hiyawa dynasts linked themselves to an ancestor with the Greek name Mopsos, it would follow that a certain Mycenean group, possibly mercenaries connected with the Sea Peoples, settled in Smooth Kilikia and established a kingdom by the tenth century BCE. Interestingly, this kingdom made use of Luwian and Phoenician as its official languages, reflecting both the dominant population of the area and the role of Phoenicians in transregional politics and economics at the time.[279]

The debate over the geographical origins of *Hiyawa* aside, this story of origins is rife with anachronism. What is missed in efforts to find an earlier Greek strand in the communities of Pamphylia and Kilikia is the simple fact that there were no Greeks in the early first millennium. The Myceneans did speak Greek, of course, but it is unclear if they conceived of themselves as ethnically similar: the term *(Ah)hiyawa* is itself an external label in all contexts except for the kingdom in Kilikia itself. Within this kingdom, Greek was seemingly not spoken, and more importantly, the Hiyawan identity, which only applied to a part of Kilikia, did not outlive the kingdom itself, suggesting that it was a primarily political identity.[280] That Mopsos is linguistically Greek does not tell us much about how Mopsos was understood by the Hiyawan dynasts, but certainly they could not have thought he was Greek, since no such idea existed

278   Grainger 2009, 12–15; Adak 2013, 63–65.
279   Jasink and Marino 2007; Yağcı 2013; Yakubovitch 2015; Bryce 2016, 70–76; Oreshko 2018. *Contra* Salmeri 2004, 184–88; Gander 2012; Payne 2012, 44.
280   The only hint of *Hiyawa* is Herodotos' comment that the Kilikians were once called *Hypachaioi* (7.91), but by whom is unclear, as is his source for this information. It is also significant that the Danuwians, a group referred to in the Hiyawa documents and seen as representing the native Luwian population (Bryce 2016, 74–76), also did not persist as an ethnic identifier in later periods.

at that time, and it is unclear what meaning a connection with the Achaeans of the Homeric tales would have had in this region.

It may also be significant that Greek writers did not perceive the inhabitants of Kilikia, or Pamphylia, as Greek until the Hellenistic period at the earliest, and even then not straightforwardly or consistently. Herodotos sees the Pamphylians as originally Trojan (7.91) and portrays the Kilikians as a separate people. Pseudo-Skylax sees both Pamphylians and Kilikians as distinct ethnicities, while qualifying that only Holmoi and Soloi within these regions were Greek cities (101–102). Strabo implies that Aspendos and Tarsos were founded by Argives, and Soloi by Achaians and Rhodians, but otherwise implies that both regions were settled by Trojans (14.4–5).[281] It is clear from this evidence that origin stories operated at the level of the local community, rather than broader ethnic groups. That they reflected any kind of historical reality or earlier perceptions of identity and origins is questionable, to say the least. Moreover, there is no evidence to suggest an alternative origin story within Pamphylian and Kilikian communities that can be clearly linked to the supposed Mycenean settlement period, since the relationship between the kingdom of Hiyawa/Que and the city of Soloi is unknown.[282]

At the heart of theories of Greek settlement in both Pamphylia and Kilikia lies the erroneous assumption that ethnic identities are primordial and relatively unchanging, static enough for there to be objective significance in the possibility that Greek-speakers migrated into these regions and, at least in the case of Hiyawa, became a ruling elite. But if such migrants lacked a broader ethnic identity upon their arrival, became indistinguishable from earlier inhabitants both culturally and with respect to the collective identity they espoused, and even stopped speaking Greek (Kilikia) or developed a dialect that highlighted difference from other Greek speakers as much if not more than similarity (Pamphylia), then what is the value of describing such a migration, if it happened, using later ethnic terms like 'Greek' (or terms that were never used ethnically, like 'Luwian'), except to perpetuate the construction of nationalist narratives of the past?

This latter aim, if muted, and its accompanying assumptions seem to underlie most of the origin stories told by modern scholars for all of the major regions of Anatolia. 'Nations' are seen to be naturally occurring entities united by language and culture, so if we can find a language or cultural similarities to

---

281   The Aspendos-Argive connection is likely confirmed by a fourth-century BCE inscription (Stroud 1984) in which the two communities expressed kinship.
282   While it is likely that Soloi lay within the territory of Hiyawa, this does not account for the many other cities of Smooth Kilikia that also probably existed in this territory but lacked any Achaian foundation myth.

attach to an ethnic label, then this must reveal an ethnic group. The cases that contradict this assumption are too numerous to recount, and yet those few scholars who have argued instead in favor of later processes of ethnogenesis remain less influential and restricted to discussing only a few groups, such as Phrygians. There is, in short, much work to be done to reconceptualize our understanding of the origins of the peoples of Anatolia.

4 Hellenization and Other Forms of Acculturation

The region of Anatolia is frequently portrayed metaphorically as a bridge or crossroads between cultures. The image here is meant to invoke the peninsula as a site of intercultural encounters and exchange, especially between the 'West' (usually Greeks but sometimes Romans) and the 'Near East.'[283] While the metaphor can direct attention away from Anatolia itself, since one only treads on a bridge in passing, the image of externally cultural traffic also underlies investigations of the impact of outside influences on the peoples of Anatolia. While these influences vary depending on the chronological framework, one can observe a distinction in how outside influences are treated in the scholarship. Groups like the Hittites and the Phrygians are seen as becoming Anatolian, no doubt because we know little about what Hittite and Phrygian culture looked like before manifesting within an Anatolian context, but also because, consequently, they do not easily fit into the East-West binary. By contrast, Iranians, Greeks, and Romans are always understood as remaining foreign, at least until Anatolia is seen to have become fully 'Hellenized.' This interpretation, though certainly motivated by the more clearly 'Western' and 'Eastern' status of these groups, is aided by the ample evidence for Iranian, Greek, and Roman culture prior to and independent of their spread on the peninsula.

In the rest of this section, I will look at the effects of an Iranian, Greek, and Roman presence on the identities of the peoples of Anatolia. My discussion considers and challenges the traditional and ongoing tendency to view these effects through the lens of acculturation, a model that is entangled with an orientalizing binary opposition between East and West, as I have just suggested, which leads to arbitrary and ultimately unconvincing lines drawn in the sands of rather close-knit beaches. Since scholarly attention predominantly alights upon the impact of Greek culture on the communities of Anatolia, I will emphasize Hellenization in what follows, with appropriate consideration of the parallel issues of Iranianization and Romanization.

---

283 For a critique of this metaphor, see Greaves 2007, 2–4.

The question when studying any form of acculturation is what exactly we mean by concepts like Hellenization, Iranianization, or Romanization. These terms have come under fire for their imprecision, in addition to several underlying assumptions that are seen as problematic. At face value, they describe processes of becoming Greek/Iranian/Roman, but such becoming can refer to anything from identity to language to the adoption of one or more cultural elements thought to belong (originally or absolutely) to Greeks/Iranians/Romans. This potential ambiguity has become actualized in the numerous studies that employ such concepts in these various ways and without consistency across studies. We can also understand such inconsistency in terms of the emic/etic divide that has informed our critique of how the peoples of Anatolia are studied thus far: language and cultural elements are externally observable phenomena which do not necessarily bear on emic expressions of identity, although scholarly work often allows the one to bleed into the other, implicitly or explicitly.[284]

These models of cultural (and identity) change have also been criticized for imposing an unnatural binary upon the two acculturating societies, particularly when it comes to Hellenization.[285] Anatolians were never really isolated from their Greek neighbors, and cultural differences were not stark. There is no clear beginning to contact, since Anatolia and the Balkans have been enmeshed in interactions long before the peoples of either region had evolved into their historically self-conscious forms. Nor is it always easy to decide what cultural elements should be assigned to a particular society, especially when some elements have evolved as a result of interactions between societies. Finally, critics accuse these models of being Helleno-centric (or Romano-centric), since processes of change tend to be viewed as progressing unidirectionally toward becoming Greek, while any adoptions of non-Greek culture are viewed as Greek appropriations that do not impact the uniqueness of their culture.[286]

In an effort to make the term less Helleno-centric, some have turned to concepts like Homi Bhabha's hybridity and Richard White's "middle ground" as a way to emphasize reciprocal and mutual processes of influence between societies.[287] With these refinements, the acculturation model continues to have its defenders, who argue that terms like Hellenization can be salvaged as useful descriptive concepts, though many simply continue to employ the terms

---

284 See, e.g., Bru, Dumitru, and Sekunda 2021, 4–5.
285 Bonnet 2015, 19–22; Dietler 2010, 90–91.
286 Flaig 1999; Dietler 2010, 57–66; Bonnet 2019. Both Dietler and Bonnet are deeply influenced by Marshall Sahlins' work on Hawaiian societies.
287 Bhabha 1994; White 1991. Cf. Dietler 2010, 57–66, who prefers the term 'entanglement.'

without acknowledging any criticism. Proponents insist on the coherence of Greek culture, even if they admit that this has little bearing on identity, and on the value of the model for highlighting political and socio-economic disparities between a "giving" and "recipient" culture.[288] In the end, Hellenistic Anatolia becomes a paradox for modern observers, who see it as deeply Hellenized while also acknowledging the development and propagation of local traditions, thus entangling two cultures that their model insists are in binary opposition.[289]

In my own critique of Hellenization and other forms of acculturation, I will attend to this debate as it plays out (or is ignored) in studies of the relationship between foreign influence, especially Hellenic, and the identities of the peoples of Anatolia. I will first consider the question of language change, then cultural change, and finally demographic change. Criticism of rival positions and defense of key assumptions and claims rarely accompany discussions of these issues, so I will attempt to draw out the implications of the relevant studies for questions of identity and cultural change. In doing so, I consider how such studies directly or indirectly answer the following questions: did the adoption of foreign practices and cultural elements alter who Anatolian peoples were, whether making them feel (more) Greek or making them appear Greek to others? Did this adoption also lead to them feeling or appearing less Lydian, Karian, *vel sim.*? Or are these the wrong questions to be asking, framed using faulty assumptions that misrepresent and confuse the meanings ascribed to various objects, institutions, and practices?

4.1   *Language*
Etymologically, terms like Hellenization refer most literally to the spread and domination of a language in a region inhabited originally by non-native speakers, and this is a common approach to the problem of acculturation in Anatolia. Where one finds an increase in Greek writing or Greek names, one can talk about the Hellenization of the region. This approach has its roots in nineteenth-century assumptions about the link between language and national culture and continues to exert an influence on current understandings of cultural history in Anatolia thanks to its endorsement by Louis Robert, who enjoys a largely deserved status as a (if not the) godfather of Anatolian studies. Throughout his enviably copious investigation of the epigraphical and

---

288   Coherence: Michels 2010, 19–29. Disparities: Attoura 2002. Cf. Chrubasik and King 2017, 7–8.
289   For the idea of a paradox, see Savalli-Lestrade 2001, 41. She views Hellenism as the medium for these local traditions, but also insists on a Greek-indigenous binary (47).

numismatic evidence from the region, he took for granted that the appearance of Greek language and/or names was a clear sign of Hellenization.[290]

According to this logic, which resembles and shares the same pitfalls as the assumption that 'native' languages signal ethnic identity, Hellenization occurred throughout the peninsula during the Hellenistic period, when Greek became the only language used in the surviving written evidence, and for some regions in the west, even earlier. In Lydia, there was partial Hellenization in the fourth and third centuries, since the Lydian language persisted in private inscriptions and Lydian names outnumbered Greek ones. Public inscriptions came to be written exclusively in Greek, but this was a response to the presence of Alexander and the Seleukids.[291] Yet by the late Hellenistic period, traces of the Lydian language became restricted to some names, and as we have seen, Strabo claims that in his day Lydian was no longer spoken at all. Mysia is less discussed in these terms, since there was not an established writing tradition in the region in the native language, but certainly the adoption of Greek itself, along with the epigraphic habit, can be seen as a sign of Hellenization, while the names of Mysians in the late-third-century lists at Delphi show a predominance of Greek names (*FD* III.4. 132 and 134).[292]

The Hellenization of Karia is viewed along similar lines as in Lydia, but as occurring somewhat earlier. Although the Karian language was used during the Archaic period outside the region, above all in Egypt, within Karia itself writing emerged, apart from a few graffiti, only in the fifth century. Karian texts, while not abundant, persisted across the fourth century and possibly into the early third century before becoming almost fully replaced by Greek. There are indications that Karian continued to be spoken during the Hellenistic period, and possibly later, but it is difficult to trace this in any detail.[293] In parallel fashion, Karian-language names dominated during the Classical period, even in our Greek sources, before gradually being 'replaced' by linguistically Greek names in the Hellenistic centuries, with only a few Karian names, especially those linked with the Hekatomnid dynasty, continuing to show up in our evidence.[294] In both cases, the Hekatomnids are credited with the first major influx of Greek writing and nomenclature – though in the short term they also encouraged the use of the Karian script – which then accelerated after Alexander. The resulting

---

290   See below for references. Cf. Fraser & Matthews 2010, ix–x, despite acknowledging the shortcomings of this approach.
291   Gauthier 1989, 160–65; Spawforth 2001, 384–86.
292   Cf. Descat 1985.
293   Hornblower 1982, 341–44; Brixhe 1993; Marek 2013.
294   Robert 1937, 337–39; Hornblower 1982, 346–50; Piras 2010.

loss of linguistic heritage is seen as a sign that Karians had become Hellenized and had given even up their Karian identity.[295]

In Lykia, written evidence comes even later, with only brief compositions on coins and ceramics before the late fifth century. During this time and the following century, Greek and Lykian are both used, with the latter dominant. The same is true of names.[296] Meanwhile, the values espoused in both Lykian and Greek by the dynasts of Xanthos are seen to reflect Persian influence.[297] After the fourth century, the dynamic between Greek and Lykian reverses itself, and Lykian ceases to be written after the early third century at the latest, while Lykian names become the minority. This process of so-called Hellenization is attributed variously to the arrival of Greek settlers or the adoption by Lykian elites of a language of prestige and power.[298] Perhaps unsurprisingly, however, this form of Hellenization is not said to have impacted Lykian identity, which was able to locally adapt Greek language and names, and even appropriated Greek stories about Lykian history.[299] Such difference of interpretation from the Karian and Lydian cases must be attributed to the efflorescence of Lykian identity in the late Hellenistic period thanks to the formation of the Lykian League (see above).

Elsewhere in Anatolia, with the exception of Pamphylia, linguistic and onomastic Hellenization occurs only from the Hellenistic period, in large part because of lack of evidence for earlier centuries.[300] In Bithynia, Hellenistic coexistence of Greek and Thracian names, even in the royal foundations, gives way to the dominance of Greek in the Roman period.[301] Greek names outnumber Phrygian (and Celtic) ones already in the Hellenistic period, a trend that parallels the abandonment of written Phrygian in favor of Greek.[302] Likewise, Greek came to dominate written texts in Hellenistic Galatia and Kilikia.[303] The same process was taking place in Pisidian cities like Termessos by the second

---

295 Bresson 2007a, 217–27; Herda 2013, 472. See, however, Aubriet 2013 for the argument that the onomastic evidence shows a resistance to Hellenization in the fourth century.
296 Schürr 2007.
297 Bousquet 1975, followed by Le Roy 1989. Cf. Demargne 1974.
298 Bryce 1990, 535–41; Le Roy 1989; Keen 1998, 175. More cautiously, Rutherford 2002; Colvin 2004; Schuler 2019.
299 Language/Names: Colvin 2004; Payne 2006, 126–34; Marek 2013, 241–43. Stories: Kolb 2014.
300 Pamphylian cities are seen as Hellenizing in the fourth century by Grainger 2009, 57–67. Yet see the increase in non-Greek (and non-Roman) names during the imperial period at Phaselis: Adak 2013, 67–78.
301 Fernoux 2004, 73–93; Marek 2009, 36–37. Cf. Fernoux 2013.
302 Brixhe 2013; Thonemann 2013, 15–24.
303 Galatia: Strobel 2002, 18–19; Kilikia: Salmeri 2011.

century BCE, though as late as the third century CE settlements in northern Pisidia still retained a dominant 'indigenous' naming practice.[304] Even later was the Hellenization of Paphlagonia, dating to the Roman period.[305]

When viewed together, these accounts of Hellenic acculturation in Anatolia reveal the inconsistencies behind concepts like Hellenization. The use of Greek language and names means a loss of Karian identity, but not of Lykian, Lydian, or Galatian identity, where one must envision a coexistence of Greek and indigenous identities.[306] For other regions, the impact of language change on identity is left unspecified; implicitly, their inhabitants have become Greek, but are they still Phrygian, Pisidian, or Paphlagonian? Only if they still spoke their native languages, it seems.[307] Yet we have already seen in the first section that language was rarely a clear marker of ethnic identity. I have argued elsewhere that the coexistence of Greek and local writing traditions in Karia suggests that neither was entrenched before the full adoption of Greek, which makes it unlikely that such language choice was a statement of ethnicity, particularly because Greek was a transregional means of communication and prestige.[308] Similar arguments have been made with regard to Lykia – though Lykian predominates to a much greater extent than elsewhere – and can also be applied to Lydia and Pamphylia.[309] For these coastal areas, the long history of contact with Greek-speakers predating the Hellenistic and even Classical periods also speaks against viewing Greek as a foreign language. Greek was familiar, even for those who did not speak it fluently, and the fact that communities made use of it for their public documents means that its associations transcended ethnic boundaries.[310] By the Hellenistic period it had become so common (*koinê*) that its origin likely did not matter, especially in those regions in which people had begun to use Greek before the imperial dominance of the Hellenistic kingdoms. An easy analogy here is modern English, spoken and written throughout the world without an accompanying feeling of being Anglicized (or Americanized).

---

304   Van Nijf 2010; Brixhe 2016, 143–46.
305   Mitchell 2010, 106–109. Discussion of linguistic or onomastic Hellenization for other regions in Anatolia is all but non-existent.
306   In addition to the citations in the preceding notes, see Kolb 2018, 81–82. On the Galatians, see Strobel 1996, 124.
307   Mitchell 1993, 172–76; Brixhe 2016 (on Pisidia only).
308   LaBuff 2013.
309   For Lykia, see Prost 2007, 107–08.
310   Cf. Frézouls 1991, 126–28. Those boundaries (Greek/non-Greek) were probably not at the forefront of ancient minds in these contexts.

The Helleno-centric privileging of the Greek language as a shaper of identity and culture becomes clearer when we compare how the evidence for Aramaic and Latin in Anatolia is treated. The use of these languages is simply seen as a product of Achaemenid and Roman imperialism without any real social or cultural consequences. Iranian and Latin names might suggest an influx of colonizers or the adoption of imperial identities by some members of the local elite, but this is rarely spoken of in terms like Iranianization or Romanization.[311] Of course, one could argue that this is because these languages and naming traditions remain rarely used in comparison to Greek (or in a few cases, local languages), but this is to ignore how any presence of Greek language or names is often seen as Hellenization. Most importantly, all of this discussion fails to link the evidence to actual expressions of identity.

4.2 *Culture*

Acculturation most literally refers to cultural assimilation, and the elements that are involved in most accounts of Hellenization typically fall into one of four complementary categories. The first of these is perhaps the only one that speaks directly to the question of identity, namely the adoption of 'Greek' stories about the past (mytho-histories) as part of a people's own history. Since a sense of a shared past represents an important aspect of Smith and Hall's theory of ethnicity, the adoption of stories that link an Anatolian people to one or more Greek peoples (see above) can lead to the argument that these Anatolians became, or at least sought to become, Greek. Yet even where Anatolians adopted Greek tales about themselves that did not imply Greekness, one often talks about Hellenization in the sense of adopting a peculiarly Greek historical mindset, either abandoning a more 'indigenous' way of thinking about one's past or simply developing this mindset where nothing had existed before. Yet such an interpretation has not gone unquestioned, particularly the assumption that the myths endorsed by Anatolian peoples are inherently and uniquely Greek. Let us look at the specifics.

In the case of Lydia, we have already seen the presence of eponymous ancestors in Xanthos' histories. This same author also tells a local version of the story of Niobe (F20), which can be seen as a Lydian appropriation of Greek myth, even as it aims to correct it. Much later, in the early first century CE, Sardis claimed kinship – a claim usually based on some mythic genealogical link – with Athens.[312] This claim may have had something to do with the fact

---

311 Marek 2009.
312 *CIG* 3456; *IGR* IV 1515.

that already in the preceding century Sardis was a member of the *koinon* of Greeks in Asia and considered itself in later centuries as the metropolis of both the Greeks and Lydians.[313]

Sardis' membership in an explicitly Hellenic community of cities is a clear sign that this core of Lydian identity had indeed become Greek, while still perpetuating Lydianness.[314] Yet this development is surprisingly late, given the switch to Greek language by the early Hellenistic period, when other aspects of Greek culture were also imported (see below). The assumption is often that the adoption of language and other cultural elements contributed to a rise in feelings of Greekness, but one wonders if politics was more of a factor – i.e., status within the Roman province of Asia, which no longer treated provincial capitals as more subordinate than 'free' cities.

Discussions of Hellenization in Mysia tend to focus almost exclusively on Pergamon under the Attalids. The dynasty's use of the Telephos myth in particular is seen both as an appeal to local Mysian history – but here it is also noted that such history originates with Greek authors – and a Greek past embedded in Telephos' homeland of Arcadia. Because the Greek Telephos became king of Teuthrania, the legendary equivalent to Mysia, Scheer reads his story as symbolizing a colonizing Hellenization of Mysia, particularly when it was incorporated into the physical and monumental landscape of the Mysian 'capital' of Pergamon.[315] Alternatively, Kuttner argues that the Attalids employed the myth to negotiate the tensions arising from the settlement of Macedonians in Pergamon, with Greek artistic style and mythical content as an 'international' rather than ethnically charged set of symbols. In her view, appeals to Greek heritage concerned the dynasty but not necessarily its subjects.[316] After the Attalids, the city became part of the same *koinon* of Greeks that Sardis joined (*Milet* I.2 #3), but whether this was based on the myth of Telephos or only stemmed from the Hellenistic influx of Greek-speakers remains uncertain. Even less clear is whether Pergamon's Greek credentials reflected upon other Mysian communities.

In addition to believing in eponymous ancestors like Kar and Chrysaor, Karian communities also participated to a great extent in kinship diplomacy with traditionally Greek cities both near and far during the Hellenistic period. Much has been made, for example, of Mylasa's claim to be related to the Kretans as an indication of Hellenization, since the city also introduced a cult

---

313 Spawforth 2001, 384–92.
314 Spawforth 2001.
315 Scheer 1993, 71–152, 338; cf. Dignas 2012.
316 Kuttner 2005.

to "Kretan-born" Zeus around this time, along with Euromos and Amyzon.[317] By the first century, Mylasa, Alabanda, and Aphrodisias were all members in the Greek *koinon* discussed above, leading many scholars to assume that this represented the culmination of a hellenizing process in which the kinship claims from earlier centuries played an important role. Yet this conclusion is less overwhelming than it at first seems. For one, the earliest kinship claim involving the Alabandeans depicted them as Chrysaoreans sharing kinship with Greeks (*OGIS* 234), thus maintaining an ethnic distinction. Second, kinship involving Krete likely appealed to a myth of migration that pre-dated the Hellenic (i.e., Dorian) stage of the island's own history. The stories behind these kinship ties invoke international connections, but not necessarily ethnic commonality.[318] Our ability to connect this diplomacy to later expressions of Greekness thus seems tenuous. The context of Roman power and, above all, the propaganda of 'Greek freedom' that surrounded the Mithridatic Wars, which immediately preceded the establishment of the Greek *koinon*, seems to matter more than any gradual developments.[319]

In Lykia, kinship diplomacy with 'Greek' cities was rarer, nor were Lykian communities involved in the Greek *koinon* of Asia, since Lykia remained nominally independent until the reign of the Roman emperor Tiberius. Nevertheless, one of the most famous inscriptions involving diplomatic kinship ties, between the cities of Xanthos and Kytenion, is often adduced as a prime example of Hellenization, since we find a Dorian town proposing kinship with a Lykian city.[320] Moreover, the more general use of 'Greek' myths by Lykian communities and writers as the basis for Lykian history is taken as a sign that Lykians inherited their own past from the Greeks.[321] The same conclusion has been asserted for Bithynians – based largely on the work of local historians – Paphlagonians (at least their dynasts), the Pisidian cities that claimed kinship with Sparta, and the Pamphylian and Kilikian cities that claimed descent from legendary Argive heroes or the seer Mopsos.[322] In most of these interpretations, Greekness accommodates or complements, rather than replaces, local traditions and identities.

---

317   Unwin 2017, 137–49, 190–207; Savalli-Lestrade 2010, 136–42.
318   Cf. Chaniotis 2009.
319   Cf. Ferrary 2001 and 2011.
320   Ma 2003, 9–12, 19–20; Erskine 2005, 126–28.
321   Heller 2009; Kolb 2014.
322   Bithynians: Fernoux 2004, 43; M. Dana 2016 and 2020, 41–44. Paphlagonians: Mitchell 2010, 92–96. Pisidians: Mitchell 1991, 25–26; Arroyo-Quirce 2016. Pamphylians and Kilikians: Scheer 1993, 179–345; López-Ruiz 2009; Oettinger 2010.

The challenge to this interpretation stems from a refusal to accept the inherent Greekness of the myths that have come down to us. For example, heroes like Bellerophon, cast in Homer and on Geometric Korinthian pottery as a 'Greek' from Korinth who migrated to Lykia and became king over the inhabitants, are instead seen as potentially derived from earlier Anatolian (Luwian) traditions.[323] Connections are also drawn between Telephos and Telepinu from Hittite mythology.[324] Salmeri has even argued that Mopsos, whose name is linguistically Greek, should be understood as a local Kilikian ruler incorporated by Greek writers into their stories.[325] What all of these counterpoints have in common is an understanding of the Eastern Mediterranean as a site for exchange of 'historical knowledge' that results in a synthesis within Greek-language writings of a variety of different strands of tradition. As Greek became the shared language of historical expression, as well as ethnography, it no longer (if it ever did) constituted the unique possession of ethnic Greeks. Instead, a variety of local and regional communities were able to stake out their distinctiveness through this discourse. Only in specific contexts, mostly tied to the *koinon* of Greeks in Asia or Hadrian's pan-Hellenion, did Greekness explicitly come into play.[326] Rather than connecting and generalizing from a few dots, it seems more in line with ancient mythic discourse to avoid labeling it as quintessentially Greek.

A second category of cultural Hellenization involves the adoption of *polis*-style communities and their accompanying institutions by the peoples of Anatolia, to be distinguished from the growth of such institutions as a result of migration and colonization, covered in the next subsection. Such adoption is often seen as a much deeper form of acculturation than the spread of other cultural elements like artistic and architectural forms because driven by a desire for autonomy that was a specifically Greek value.[327] Thus, the establishment of *polis* institutions by Sardis after its re-founding under Antiochos I is viewed as a key moment in the city's acquisition of Greekness, and eventual autonomy after Apameia, alongside its continued Lydian identity.[328] The fourth-century urbanization of western Karia in the fourth century represented a conscious emulation – encouraged by the Hekatomnids – of Ionia

---

323 On Geometric depictions of Bellerophon, see Ziskowski 2014. On the possible Anatolian origin/contribution to this figure, see Le Roy 2004, esp. 8 n.6; Raimond 2007; Bachvarova 2015, 146–50.
324 Stewart 1996, 109–19.
325 Salmeri 2004.
326 On the pan-Hellenion, see Romeo 2002.
327 Most recently, Mitchell 2017.
328 Kosmin 2019; Gauthier 1989, 151–70.

and other Greek cities, a way of life incompatible with the region's "wild interior," which was dominated by villages and temple-states.[329] In Lykia, the adoption of *polis* institutional forms produced Hellenization, or Karianization if imposed by the Hekatomnids, that contributed to the emergence of a common Lykian identity.[330] The urbanization of Bithynia, first under Lysimachos and the Bithynian monarchs, then through Pompey's interventions here and in Paphlagonia and Pontos, is a more contested development, with some inferring Hellenization, even when driven by Roman leaders. Others prefer a term like modernization to describe this process, arguing that most of the Greek institutions involved were already present beforehand.[331]

In Pisidia, the emergence of urbanized, autonomous city-states during the Hellenistic period is also described as Hellenization, since these communities are depicted as seeking a particularly Greek form of public life and self-governance, while remaining ethnically Pisidian.[332] A similar institutional 'self-Hellenization' is envisioned for the late Hellenistic cities of Kappadokia, embodied by the now famous inscription published by the citizens of Hanisa (Kanesh) in the second century BCE.[333] And the greater urbanization in Smooth Kilikia represents a Hellenic stamp lacking in the more isolated mountains of Rough Kilikia.[334]

In these discussions we witness inconsistency or vagueness about what Hellenization actually means: in some studies, it comes close to referring to a shift in identity, while for others communities can institutionally hellenize without becoming Greek. This latter conclusion has the merit of avoiding the topic of identity where no direct evidence suggests it, but leaves open the question of what conceptual work 'Hellenization' is actually doing. For many, it describes a process of self-conscious emulation of Greek political forms and ideals, but this is a dangerous inference. The similarity between Aegean *poleis* and those that arise beyond the western and (to some extent) northern coasts of Anatolia from the fourth century onwards is undeniable; but to assign Greekness to autonomy and these institutions goes well beyond the evidence. For one, it

---

329 Marchese 1989; Chrubasik 2017, 88–107. Less value-laden but essentially similar views are expressed by Carpenter and Boyd 1977 and Debord 2005.
330 Kolb 2003. For the view that these institutions were imposed by the Hekatomnids, see Domingo Gygax 2001, 67–122.
331 Hellenization: Marek 2009, 38–40. Modernization: Michels 2009, 253–89; cf. Michels 2013.
332 Mitchell 1991/1992; Vanhaverbeke and Waelkens 2005; Labarre et al. 2015. Cf. Vandorpe 2000, 498–500.
333 Robert 1963, 471–79; Michels 2013; cf. Michels 2009, 339–50.
334 Desideri 1991; cf. Sayar 2004.

ignores the clear traditions of autonomy in most places in Anatolia, from the concerted actions of Karians during the 'Ionian' revolt to the challenges faced by the Persians in controlling certain areas of Mysia, Pisidia, and northeastern Anatolia. This position turns an even blinder eye to the unambiguous evidence that there was not in antiquity a fixed notion of what a *polis* was institutionally or ethnically. Our sources apply the term to a variety of institutional arrangements and do not bat an eye at calling a number of non-Greek cities *poleis* even in the Classical period. The modern tendency to equate the *polis* with Greekness is, therefore, a product of more recent historiographical demons, rooted in nineteenth century nationalism.[335] Once we recognize this, then the fact that urbanizing communities modeled their institutions on nearby urban communities becomes just that: a response to growth by mirroring settlements who have already achieved that growth in the past and developed appropriate institutions. The goals of autonomy and urbanism were, if not universal, certainly not the property of one ethnic group.

A second candidate for institutional Hellenization involves the indigenous or Iranian dynasties ruling the independent kingdoms of Hellenistic Anatolia, especially those of Bithynia, Pontos, and Kappadokia. Here attention is paid to the participation of some or all of these rulers in 'Greek' practices of diplomacy and benefaction, the construction of courts of 'friends,' and the patronage of Hellenic forms of *paideia*. In short, these kings are seen as imitating the 'models' of Hellenistic kingship in Alexandria, Antioch, and Macedon.[336] The Attalid kings, despite their potentially non-Greek ancestry and Anatolian base of power, are rarely grouped with these other monarchies because the early rulers, according to the standard view, sought to "clean up their own origins."[337]

Recently, several studies have shown that views of these courts as 'Hellenized' are problematic, pointing out their heterogeneous nature and even arguing that Greek aspects were not dominant, especially in the 'Iranian' dynasties of Pontos and Kappadokia. These last two cases also raise the question of Iranianization, with "Magian" learning and, in Kappadokia, a prevalence of Iranian

---

335   Vlassopoulos 2007, esp. 77–84, 101–22, 190–202. The consistent usage argued by Hansen & Nielsen 2004, 29–46 does not encompass specific institutions.
336   Bithynia: Vitucci 1953, 127–30; Hannestad 1996; M. Dana 2020, 44–54; cf. Michels 2009, 29–36. Pontos: Olshausen 1974; Savalli-Lestrade 1998, 242–45; Ballesteros Pastor 2006, 381–86 and 2020, 8–11. Kappadokia: Michels 2020.
337   Kosmetatou 2003 (quote on 167, referring more so to the stigmatized social position of Philetairos, a eunuch, and his mother, apparently a prostitute); Gruen 2000. A contemporary poet was crucified for mocking the Attalids, calling them "scraps of Lysimachos' treasure, rulers of Lydians and Phrygia" (Strabo 14.1.39). Cf. Weber 1998–1999, 165–67.

onomastics among the courtiers.[338] Yet here the relationship between Iranian and indigenous, which tend to be conflated without justification, remains unexplored. In any case, returning to the question of Hellenized courts, it represents the height of conceptual flexibility to call this institution, which witnessed many new developments alongside certain continuities with the Classical Macedonian and Persian monarchies, Greek.[339] This overall new form of monarchy represented adoption and adaptation for all parties involved.

A final instance of institutional acculturation is derived from the impact of Rome on Anatolia. Besides continued 'Hellenization' in the form of urbanization of the peninsula's interior, a 'Romanization' of elites is also envisioned.[340] In a now classic article, Greg Woolf argues that the civilizing logic of Roman conquest and rule sought to impose order on the Greeks, which included Hellenized Anatolians, by keeping them from their own vices.[341] His focus on the Roman literary perspective leaves little room for consideration of what this form of Romanization looked like on the ground, but this question has been recently (if selectively) addressed by a few studies. First, Devijver explores social promotion into the equestrian and senatorial classes of local Sagalassian elites as a form of Romanization, yet the question of how this impacted the broader community is left unaddressed.[342] Mitchell's briefer consideration of the issue suggests that claims to Roman (political) identity through naming practices was limited to the upper-echelons of civic society.[343] Second, Eckhardt studies the professional associations in Roman Phrygia, which he argues were encouraged by certain statutes in Roman law. He too focuses less on questions of identity and more on Romanization as simply "the changes brought about by Roman rule." It remains unclear to me why this phrase cannot suffice to refer to such changes, rather than employing a term like Romanization that carries connotations of identity transformation even when not intended. At the same time, Eckhardt also rejects the idea that these developments emanated from the Roman ideological discourse studied by Woolf.[344]

---

338   Gabelko 2017; Ballesteros Pastor 2020.
339   See, e.g., Engels 2017.
340   On urbanization of the interior, see, e.g., Mitchell 2000, 126–32.
341   Woolf 1994, 118–25; cf. Woolf 2010.
342   Devijver 1996. He also asserts that such Romanization could only occur among "Hellenized" elites steeped in *paideia*, but fails to provide substantial evidence for this claim, other than the use of the Greek language.
343   Mitchell 2000, 131–32.
344   Eckhardt 2016. See also the slightly more nuanced but evasive treatment of Roman Lykia by Kolb 2007.

Thirdly, we must consider the question of religion. Here perhaps more than any other cultural element, we witness the employment of the bridge/crossroads metaphor, for example in the recent survey of Anatolian religion by Christian Marek.[345] Greek (Western) influence dates to the Classical period, when regions near coastal Greek settlements referred to their gods with Greek names: Artemis in Sardis, Zeus and Artemis in Karia, Apollo in Lykia.[346] Even in their native languages, Anatolians may have worshiped gods whose names derive from Greek, such as Lydian Lews (Zeus), Lamêtrus (Demeter) and Paki (Bacchos), or Lykian Ertemi, Pedrita (Aphrodite) and Leththi (Leto).[347] The fifth and fourth centuries are also seen as a time of Iranianization for the cults of Kappadokia.[348] With the spread and dominance of the Greek language in the hellenistic period, most regions adopted the nomenclature of the Greek pantheon for most of their gods, incorporated older cults as part of the institutions of the *polis*, and at times even imported new gods such as 'Kretan-born' Zeus in Karia.[349] The exceptions seem to highlight the overall trend to adopt a hellenized visual and conceptual framework for Anatolian cults. The widespread worship of the Mother Goddess and Men, as well as more localized cults in East Lydia, Sinuri in Karia, the protector gods in Pisidia, or Sandan in Kilikia are seen as indigenous remnants preserved amidst, but often also altered by, the general tide of religious Hellenization.[350] Complementary to this interpretation is the inclusion of Persian and Levantine (Eastern) influences, so that by the Roman imperial period, Anatolia had become a "dense, multicolored fabric" of indigenous and external traditions from both east and west, where each cult is to be understood in terms of the ethnic tradition it belongs to.

In tracking this kind of acculturation, most scholars recognize that the simple use of a Greek name for a deity is not a guarantee of Hellenization, since this could just represent a translation of an indigenous cult, often described with the ambiguous phrase *interpretatio graeca*. The storm-god Tarhunt in

---

345 Marek 2016, 508–25, implementing the framework of Keil 1923.
346 Sardis: Payne & Wintjes 2016, 97–100 (but more cautiously, Payne 2019, 233). Karia: Sears 2014, 213–17.
347 Lydian: Payne & Wintjes 2016, 103–106; Lykian: Bryce 1986, 183–84 and 1990, 531–34; Keen 1998, 61–70; Le Roy 2004.
348 Michels 2017, 45–47.
349 Lydia: de Hoz 1999; Marqués (2019) sees even the Hellenistic worship of Kybele as a form of Hellenization through incorporation into a *polis* framework. Karia: Hornblower 1982, 344–46; Savalli-Lestrade 2010, 144–46. Pisidia: Mitchell 1991, 144–45 (= 1992, 25–26). Kilikia: Pohl 2004a.
350 Mother Goddess: Roller 1991; East Lydian cults: de Hoz 1999, esp. 10, 125–26; Men: Labarre 2009; Sinuri: Robert 1945; Williamson 2016. Pisidian gods: Robert 1962, 218–19; Akıncı Öztürk and Malay 2012. Sandan: Pohl 2004b.

Kilikia becomes Zeus and the Mother Goddess in Lykia becomes Leto without either ceding their native character. The Lykian examples lead Kolb to infer merely terminological changes, against Bryce's earlier claim that 'Leto' was a colonization of the native Lykian goddess.[351] At the same time, attestations of Artemis (Lyd. *artimu-*) in Sardis are early enough that many see this deity as emerging in an Anatolian milieu shared by Ionians and Lydians.[352] Even a god like Men, whose name seems to root him in an Iranian religious milieu, has been shown to have much stronger connections to Anatolia.[353]

Forms of worship that appear to be modelled on Greek practices, such as the subordination of cults to *polis* institutions or the introduction of new 'Greek' cults, may seem better candidates for the label Hellenization. The former, however, depends on the assumption that the *polis* was peculiarly Greek, a preconception we have already called into question. The incorporation of older cults into a *polis* framework is symptomatic of evolving notions of communal identity and place within a broader world in response to processes like urbanization and the growth of international contacts. More important to questions of cultural change and identity is the fact that the focus of these cults continues to be the articulation of the community's relationship with local landscapes. As for the importation of new cults, often this reflected a new group of settlers (see next subsection) but where this is unlikely or uncertain, as with the cult of Kretan-born Zeus in Karia, it would be odd to invoke Hellenization when such a cult was not practiced anywhere else besides Krete itself.[354] The argument that anything in 'Greece' is 'Greek' glosses over the extreme diversity of the Greek religious landscape and imposes a fundamental link between cult and myth – in assuming the religious importance of the Kretan birthplace of Zeus – inspired more by a Judeo-Christian mindset than a study of ancient religion on its own terms.

One religious phenomenon worth considering is the spread of competitive festivals during the Hellenistic and Roman periods, whose Greek orientation is often indicated by the claim at this time that such competitions were 'isolympic' or 'isopythic.' This spread has only been studied as a sign of Hellenization (and where gladiator shows are involved, of Romanization) for northern Anatolia, and so represents an opportunity for further study.[355] In particular, it should be considered to what extent such festivals also expressed local forms

---

351   Kolb 2003, 237; Bryce 1990, 531–34.
352   De Hoz 1999, 11–14, and 2016; Payne 2019, 233. Cf. Hönigmann and Oettinger 2018, 74–80.
353   Labarre 2009.
354   Unwin 2017, 190–207.
355   Marek 2003, 95–103 and 2009, 41–43.

of identity in a global milieu, rather than assuming that the similarities mattered more in establishing a uniformly Greek culture.[356]

I end this subsection with a consideration of other cultural elements that tend to be seen as signs of Hellenization and, more rarely, Romanization.[357] Related to religion are the forms of architecture that came to shape the construction of sanctuaries in Anatolia from the fourth-century onwards. The Hekatomnid monumentalization of several major sanctuaries in Karia based on a Greek temple model represents for many scholars a form of Hellenization, with the specifically 'Karian' appropriation of this model serving merely as a byproduct of the spread of Greek culture.[358]

In the realm of private architecture, burial evidence shows clear signs of foreign influence, for example the Maussolleion and the monumental tombs from Lykia. Dusinberre's important synthesis of the evidence from western Anatolia (especially Lydia, Karia, and Lykia) leads her to conclude that elites incorporated Mesopotamian or Persian forms into their tomb architecture to express an Achaemenid political identity/status, while maintaining more local forms of ethnic identity.[359] The study of Sardis' Hellenistic ceramics has resulted in similar conclusions.[360] Along these lines, recent interpretations of the Maussolleion (and other dynastic tombs in Karia) push against the earlier tendency to focus on the monument as a product of the Hellenizing program of the Hekatomnid dynasty, instead preferring to view this and other Hekatomnid monuments through the lens of Creolization. In this view, the mixture of local and foreign styles served to normalize a dynastic tradition in the region and define a regional Karian identity.[361] Dusinberre's conclusions also challenge earlier work on Lykia, which claimed that initial resistance to "polis ideology" gave way after 400 BCE to architecture and art on tombs that replaced the older preference for "oriental" themes with Greek ones.[362]

Beyond these western regions, scholarship remains comfortable with the Hellenization model to account for the Archaic importation of Greek ceramics in Kilikia, the adoption of Greek funerary architecture and literary epitaphs in

---

356   For example, the discussion of the foundation of music festival in second-century CE Oinoanda by Mitchell 2000, 130–31 tendentiously assumes the "hellenic" (*sic*) character of the festival because it excluded the regionally popular wrestling event.
357   For a consideration of grave architecture as a sign of Romanization, see Schörner 2005.
358   Pedersen 2013.
359   Dusinberre 2013. Cf. Carstens 2009, 52–62; Baughn 2010 and Dusinberre 2019 on Lydia.
360   Berlin 2019.
361   Earlier interpretation: Hornblower 1982, 332–39. Recent interpretation: Carstens 2009; Prost 2013; Henry 2013b.
362   Demargne 1974; cf. Keen 1998, 58–70.

the Bithynian countryside, the burial practices and dining habits of Galatians, and the construction of *gymnaseia* other 'Greek' public buildings throughout the region after Alexander.[363] Yet the approach of situating such products within their local and sociopolitical contexts that is now being applied to religious and funerary architecture should also be taken when interpreting this evidence.[364] How Greek cultural forms contributed to status within these contexts, beyond the simple assertion that an elite was involved, remains an open question that tends to be overshadowed by an emphasis on a vaguely defined 'Hellenization.' Were these (to us) 'Greek' cultural elements signs of a Hellenic cultural identity to the consumers and patrons behind their creation?

That this question is rarely considered can be illustrated by a brief discussion of the inference that the presence of a *gymnasion* in a formerly non-Greek community equates to deep cultural (and self-pursued) Hellenization.[365] This conclusion is largely based on the clear associations with an education modelled on that of Greek *poleis* that these buildings have. There is, however, a double-standard and inconsistent logic applied to interpretations of the spread of this institution in Hellenistic Anatolia (and other parts of the 'East'). For one, the absence of *gymnaseia* in traditionally 'Greek' cities on the western coast does not lead to claims that, when such buildings were constructed later on, these cities became Hellenized, yet this is precisely the opposite conclusion reached when discussing non-Greek cities who built a *gymnasion*. By the same token, if only two of these buildings are attested in Asia Minor in the fourth century, and one of these is Karian Mylasa, then we need to rethink the insistence that this institution was peculiarly Greek and a requirement for *poleis*.[366] Secondly, most of the education that took place in a *gymnasion* involved local civic and religious knowledge. In other words, while we can identify formalistic similarities, the content of gymnastic education was always different because it was

---

363   Kilikian ceramics: Aslan 2011; Bithynian funerary structures: Fernoux 2004, 95–111; M. Dana 2020, 54–65. Galatian culture: Strobel 2002, 18–37; Public Buildings: Groß-Albenhausen 2004 (gymnaseia only); van Nijf 2010, 175–77 (on Termessos); Rens 2015 (on Pisidia).

364   Such an approach has yielded convincing conclusions when it comes to the use of Greek-style coins in Kilikia, attributed to economic rather than acculturating motives by Meyer 2004.

365   See, e.g., the discussions of Toriaion's request to be allowed to build a *gymnasion* by Bringmann 2004 and Alonso Troncoso 2009.

366   An example of this inconsistent, even contradictory logic, comes from Daubner 2015, who insists that the institution served to preserve Greekness in the eastern colonies, while admitting (but ignoring) the dearth of evidence for gymnasia in most of these colonies. Along similar lines, he claims that the lack of a *gymnaseion* in a 'Greek' city does not mean that there were no spaces for 'gymnastic' activities, but the same assumption is never made for non-Greek cities.

based on local communal identities, and I suspect that content mattered more in how the possession and functioning of a *gymnasion* was understood, especially with respect to group identities.

4.3   Migration and Colonization

A final impetus for acculturation is the presence and impact of settlers from areas in which the culture in question originated. It is in this sense that the question of Iranianization receives its fullest treatment, in conjunction with the Achaemenid grants of royal land to Iranian elites in Anatolia. Debate centers on the nature of these grants and the system of land tenure they imply, but there is general agreement that such settlements, which must have involved the appropriation of relatively large estates from indigenous individuals or groups, were concentrated in specific areas and did not dominate the Anatolian landscape generally. They seem most prevalent in areas near satrapal capitals, unsurprisingly, or on isolated estates that became linked with or even incorporated into nearby Anatolian communities. Such settlements may have contributed to the spread of Achaemenid cult and material culture mentioned above, but overall did not lead to a long-lasting or deeply rooted Iranianization.[367]

The region of Kappadokia, including the Pontic north, is a different matter. The fact that the Hellenistic dynasties that came to rule here boasted an Achaemenid lineage, along with the Iranian names of both the rulers and many of the elite, has produced the supposition that this elite was the product of earlier Achaemenid land grants.[368] The issue remains understudied, however. Our sources portray the elite under the Ariarathids as Kappadokian, and do not assign an ethnicity to their Pontic counterparts. Moreover, if the elite were Iranian, then the presence of Iranian cultural elements that were likely restricted to the elite does not represent acculturation at all.

Turning to Hellenic settlement, the issue is of course complicated by the fact that Western Anatolia was home to Greek-speaking peoples before the rise of Greekness as a self-conscious identity or coherent culture – the murkiness of the migrations that resulted in such communities precludes any ability to discuss a cultural impact until much later.[369] As discussed above, it is more accurate to refer to a Greco-Anatolian cultural milieu in Archaic western Anatolia than to distinguish Greek and non-Greek culture in the region, or to posit similarity in terms of a one-way process of dissemination rather than

---

367 Briant 1985; Sekunda 1985, 1988, 1990; Schuler 1998, 147–53. Cf. Casabonne 2004, 93–97 on Kilikia.
368 Michels 2017, 44–45; Mitchell 2007.
369 On this murkiness, see Rose 2008 and Mac Sweeney 2017.

reciprocal exchange.[370] The same can be said for the supposed Early Iron Age 'Greek' settlement in Pamphylia and Kilikia, which is posited to explain the presence of a distinct Greek dialect in the former, and the Mycenean political origins of the kingdom Hiyawa in the latter (see above). In both cases, we cannot speak of Hellenization when there was no coherent Greek identity, culture, or even language (understood at the time). The brief rise in 'Greek' ceramics in Archaic Kilikia is likewise indicative of economic contacts and elite consumption practices but certainly not feelings of identity.[371]

More impactful perhaps was the colonization of the northern coast during the Archaic period, a historically attested set of settlements like Herakleia, which saw itself as a Milesian colony and, as we have seen, came to enslave the indigenous Mariandynians. Yet this example suggests that, to the extent that Greekness mattered in such contexts, ethnic distinctions that determined social status trumped any efforts to assimilate non-Greeks.[372]

For most of Anatolia, then, the question of Hellenization arises in the context of Hellenistic and, to a lesser extent, Roman-era colonization. In Getzel Cohen's survey of Hellenistic foundations, he counts 136 possible cases in regions that previously were dominated by non-Greek Anatolian peoples, out of which 115 are certain or probable. Of these, Macedonian settlers are indicated for only 23, the vast majority of which (17) are located in either Lydia or Phrygia. To this count we should add Sagalassos in Pisidia.[373] Only five (three in Phrygia) show clear signs of Greek settlement. By contrast, non-Greek settlers from elsewhere, especially Mysians and Thracians, are involved in seven cases.[374] At a surface level, then, the impact of these settlements would seem to be extremely limited.

A more in-depth consideration of the issue runs into several challenges. First, it is not clear to what extent Macedonians represented agents of so-called Greek culture, especially *polis* culture. Certainly, they would have aided in the spread of the Greek language, but Macedonians did not typically

---

370 Nevertheless, the argument that Ionians were originally non-Greek peoples native to Anatolia (Işik 2012; 2016, 456–57), based on a recently found inscription from fourteenth-century BCE Egypt that refers to "Great Ionia" (on which, see Haider 2008), remains untenable, since it privileges an external perspective and seeks to infer ethnic identity from a toponym. Haider's conclusion that later Greek-speaking migrants adopted a local toponym seems much more plausible.

371 Pace Yağcı 2013; cf. Aslan 2011. See also the doubts of Casabonne (2004, 89–92) that there was any Greek colonization in Kilikia before the Hellenistic period.

372 Gallotta 2005.

373 Kosmetatou and Waelkens 1997.

374 Cohen 1995, 151–409. Cf. Kosmetatou 2005 on the difficulties of identifying Macedonians in Pisidia.

organize themselves into *poleis* before the Hellenistic period, and thus the creation of communities in which standardized civic institutions determined public life would have represented a change for them as much as (and sometimes more than) their Anatolian neighbors. There is also the question of what 'Macedonian' meant to the inhabitants of a community. After the generation of the Diadochi, Billows has shown that claims of being Macedonian, whether direct or through symbols like the 'Macedonian' shield, came to emanate from ethnically diverse military units and settlers.[375] While this development on some level reflects the 'Macedonianization' of individuals in these units, it leaves open the question of whether such Macedonian identity was still ethnic or not. Many of the communities claiming this identity did so centuries later, in the Roman period: what the relationship of these claims to Roman Macedonia or Greek identity was remains assumed rather than investigated.

Even if these Macedonians can be seen as possible agents of Hellenization in Anatolia their concentration in Lydia and, to a lesser extent, Phrygia, raises a further reason for caution. Many of these Macedonian settlements are in locations where previously Iranians seem to have been granted land under the Achaemenids.[376] This coincidence does not negate the impact of these settlements as barriers to the preservation of a regionally coherent Lydian identity, as posited in the first section. Yet it also suggests that these Macedonian settlers were displacing the previous foreign elite, limiting the impact on other areas in Lydia and Phrygia. As for the rest of Anatolia, Macedonian settlements were sparse indeed.

One final point should be made about these Macedonian settlements. There is good reason to suppose that in many cases Macedonians formed communities alongside local inhabitants. This is certainly the case for Stratonikeia, a Seleukid foundation that Strabo explicitly calls Macedonian. Yet when we turn to the epigraphic evidence from the city, we learn that the major civic subdivisions were the formerly independent communities that were absorbed into the new settlement. The major deities of the city were not Macedonian imports, but the major cults of earlier times, including that of Zeus Chrysaoros, which as we have seen inspired a Karian religious federation.[377] All of this indicates a form of colonization that resulted in the valuing of earlier local traditions rather than the privileging of settler identity and culture.

---

375   Billows 1995, 147–57, 170–72.
376   Billows 1995, 147–57, 170–72.
377   Debord 2004; van Bremen 2000, 2004.

The cases where we have clear attestations of Greek settlers are not only rare, but also hardly indicative of Hellenization even in some of these cities' local environment. Settlers from Magnesia were joined by Thracians at Antiocheia by Pisidia, whose main deity, Men Askaenos, reflected local traditions and, probably, settlement.[378] The Ionian heritage of Laodikeia, expressed by the civic tribe Ias, coexisted with a community that eventually boasted its Phrygian identity on its coinage, as we have seen.[379] And Nikaia is only called Greek by Dio Chrysostom (*Or.* 39.1), an author who explores and even challenges Greek and other identities in complex and contradictory ways across his work; to take him as reflecting common understandings of identity seems unwise.[380]

It would be unfair to leave matters there, since for the majority of the Hellenistic settlements catalogued by Cohen the evidence is far from abundant, and the silence of our sources may conceal or take for granted the arrival of Greeks and Macedonians.[381] There is no denying this possibility, but there are, to my mind, good reasons to suspect that this was not the general pattern either. First, possessing 'Macedonian' heritage seems to have constituted a source of pride and/or represented significant cultural cache for communities in the Roman period, so if more communities were able to lay claim to this, why did they not choose to do so? Along these lines, when an author like Strabo chooses to explicitly label a city as Macedonian, as he does for Thyateira and Karian Stratonikeia, this seems to distinguish these Hellenistic foundations from those that he discusses without reference to Macedonians. Moreover, the large number of Macedonian settlements in Lydia corresponds to the geographer's statement that Lydia is home not only to Lydians but also Macedonians and Mysians – this latter group also shows up at sites like Gordos and Mysotimolos.

There is, of course, the possibility that some settlements welcomed Macedonians (and Greeks), but that the memory of their origins became insignificant over time to the community's identity; in such cases, their impact on the Hellenization of the community would have been limited to those cultural elements that we have already criticized as being erroneously associated with Greekness through an essentialized and Helleno-centric lens.

Finally, we should consider that many 'settlements' in Cohen's reckoning did not involve new settlers at all, but simply a renaming and, at times, rebuilding

---

378 Cohen 1995, 278–79.
379 On Ias, see Robert 1969, 325–31.
380 Jackson 2017, 222–26.
381 This is the assumption of Tempesta 2013, 36–38.

of a damaged urban infrastructure. This was the case for over half the 'settlements' in Kilikia and Karia, at sites like Tarsos/Seleukeia and Alabanda/Antiocheia.[382] It does not include foundations like Antiocheia on the Maeander and Nysa, which were the product of synoecisms of pre-existing villages. Elsewhere, examples include one of three possible cases in Lykia, the two major foundations in Kappadokia, half the cases in Pontos and Paphlagonia, and four instances in Bithynia – though in this last case older Greek cities were often involved. In almost all of these cases, the stamp of imperialism was clear, since renaming often reflected members of royal families, but as an even unintentional impetus for Hellenization, they remain questionable at best.

The Roman period was a crucial time for many communities to adapt their local traditions to broader categories of identity, especially in Lydia and Phrygia, as we have discussed several times above. But it was also the occasion for a new wave of *coloni*, especially in less urbanized areas like Pisidia or northern Anatolia.[383] The impact of these settlements tends to be viewed either as Hellenization or in minimalist terms, with small islands of Latin-speaking communities existing in an encroaching sea of Greco-Anatolians. In part this is because some Roman colonies were set up as segregated communities alongside pre-existing ones, which emphasized their different ethnic and perhaps cultural status, while others involved the absorption of the colonists into the larger civic body, which was paralleled by the subsuming of Roman culture into that of Hellenism.[384]

Where Romanization is said to have occurred as a result of these colonies, it is typically viewed in relation to Anatolians as Greeks. Sartre argues for minimal Romanization, in large part because most aspects of culture (e.g., architecture and cult) were not distinctly Roman enough to distinguish them from their Greek counterparts. Only in the case of language (which is not dominant compared to Greek) and elite status (especially citizenship) does he feel justified in speaking of Romanization.[385]

---

382 Cf. Sayar 2007 on Kilikia.
383 On the Pisidian colonies, see Syme 1995, 225–41.
384 For these trends in Pisidia, see Mitchell 1993, 89–97; in northern Anatolia, see Marek 2009, 38–39 & 43.
385 Sartre 2007.

5   Conclusion

My critique in the last section speaks to a larger strand of criticism running across this work, namely an abiding suspicion of the valence of group identities that serve as the ancient counterpart to the categories of modern nationalism or orientalist discourse. Just as the Greek/Iranian, Greek/Anatolian, or Roman/Anatolian-*qua*-Greek binaries map too easily onto the West/East terminology of the modern era, so too does the assumption that regional ethnic identities existed and were primary for ancient inhabitants of Anatolia resemble the constructs posing as descriptions that modern nationalistic ideologies produce. That ethnic identities are inferred from ancient evidence that does not consistently express itself in such terms is telling. On the one hand, texts that predominantly refer to peoples as Karians, Lydians, or Phrygians are overwhelmingly ethnographic in nature, representing an etic perspective motivated to order its material in a way that makes sense to its largely foreign (to Anatolia) readership. On the other hand, our emic perspectives generally eschew broader categories in favor of local identities.

As we have seen, sometimes broader identities did matter for Anatolians. Yet the tendency in scholarship is to implicitly assume the subordination of local identities, which are almost always attested with far greater frequency, to these broader identities. This is not to say that regional and local identities could not map onto each other: if a Selgean were asked if she was also Pisidian, she would undoubtedly say yes (unless unfamiliar with the latter term, which is entirely possible). But if asked who she was or where she was from, she would be much more likely to say Selgean or Selge, respectively. The number of Selgeans living or traveling abroad dwarfs those calling themselves Pisidians in similar contexts, a situation that contrasts sharply with the modern traveler or expat experience, where nationality almost always comes first.

In other words, just because we can speak of a Karian League or Lydian Sardis or a Bithynian kingdom does not mean that inhabitants of these regions cared more about these adjectives than being Mylasean, Sardian, or Nikomedeian. The sparse evidence for the Karian League, the late nature of evidence for explicitly Lydian expressions, and the multi-ethnic character of the Bithynian rulers' subjects all urge caution before embracing these identities as primary categories of agency and historical analysis, to be extended over language and material culture. Even more significant is my argument that many regions of Anatolia may not have been home to any ethnic community, broadly conceived. If I am right, then much of the scholarship on the peoples of Anatolia has misconstrued an exercise of *identification* as a study of an ethnic group.

Rather than uncovering a poorly understood people, they have assumed its existence (or its pervasiveness) and constructed origins, culture, and language from the patterns they hoped to find in the evidence.

Similar missteps haunt investigations of cultural encounters and their impact on Anatolians, which is less excusable given the growing body of scholarship attacking the acculturation model. The insistence on a distinctly Greek culture not only founders in the face of studies demonstrating that a shared cultural milieu between 'Greeks' and non-Greeks defined several areas of the Mediterranean, including Western Anatolia, already in the Early Iron Age, but exposes the scholarly privileging of their own constructed categories over ancient understandings of culture, language, and identity. This privileging of modern categories speaks to the overall conservative nature of the several disciplines of ancient studies (classics, ancient history, classical archaeology), but more importantly folds their practitioners into the legacy of earlier scholarship that felt more emboldened to declare both ancient Greeks and the modern West superior to their eastern counterparts.

My proposed alternative, which I can only briefly outline here, is to remember that terms like 'Lydian,' 'Bithynian,' or 'Greek' were and continue to be above all *arguments*, rather than descriptive labels, at least within discourses from or about the ancient Mediterranean. When Ziaelas called himself "King of the Bithynians," he sought to represent his position by reinforcing a notion of ethnic unity among his subjects that may have been rather weak without monarchical support – a unity that in turn helped to buttress royal claims of sovereignty. When Sardis called itself the *metropolis* of Lydia, it aimed to establish its supreme status in the region vis-à-vis Roman power by appealing to a particularly imperialistic way of understanding its past. In both examples, particular moments of regional ethnic expression clearly emanated from specific political goals, which were not pervasive aims of individuals and communities across the many centuries of antiquity. Far more often, individuals and groups promoted local identities, calling themselves Sardian or Mylasean or Nikomedeian. Perhaps it is worth considering such identities, traditionally called 'civic,' as the primary ethnicities of the peoples of Anatolia, given the central role of shared kinship myths, attachment to territory, and common history to communal identity in these cities. That we can envision, and occasionally witness, larger group identities among these local communities does not mean that such identities commanded significant loyalty of their members.[386]

---

386   See J. Hall 2015, 22 for the criterion that ethnic identity refers to the "'*largest* group to command loyalty based on felt kinship ties,'" (citing Connor 1994, 202) arguing from this that *polis* identity should not be considered ethnic in most cases. That he culls this criterion

In the same vein, when formerly non-Greek cities like Mylasa declared themselves members of the *koinon* of Greeks in Asia, they were not making explicit the conclusion of a centuries-long process of Hellenization that everyone understood had already made them objectively Greek (as if), but exploiting intertwined mythologies and (perhaps) cultural similarities with other Anatolian cities in order to gain privileged political status within a Roman province. We unfortunately know nothing of the developments leading up to the league, but it is even possible, if my suggestion is correct that the 'Greek' label for the *koinon* came from the Romans, that urbanism mattered more than anything else. I suspect that if Greekness was significant in a pervasive and consistent way across time, it would have been policed to a much greater extent. Instead, what we find is a discourse of peer polity interaction (and its associated behaviors) driving the evolution of local communities in ways that led to greater similarities, especially in language, political institutions, and urban material culture, that were only occasionally (and strategically) conceptualized as 'Greek.' Meanwhile, local traditions continued to distinguish these communities as well, which in fact informed their identities to a greater extent than the growing similarities, judging by the evidence. When we privilege the occasional over the frequent, we are making an argument that is far from impartial or innocuous about the importance of the rarer term.

As these comments hopefully recall, my intention is to challenge how we conduct studies of the peoples of Anatolia. As described at the outset, most such studies tend to focus on one or at most two of these peoples, and given the complexities of the evidence, that will likely (and should) continue. At the same time, I think there is great value, if also dangers, in employing a peninsula-wide framework, as Christian Marek has already shown in his monumental opus focusing on the political history of the region. This value lies first of all in the revelation that approaches to regional studies are more obviously problematic when we look at their inconsistent (or consistently erroneous) results. Another potential benefit is the posing of new questions for study. Why do some regions develop ethnic communities while others do not? Why does the Roman period witness the renewal or birth of ethnic communities in such contrast to the preceding period(s)? My brief explanations above are at best the first word on subjects that merit substantial loquacity. Finally, an Anatolian framework allows us to test the possibility that there is something distinctly

---

from a work on modern ethno-nationalism reveals his own anachronistic bias, along with a certain circularity, since he defends the criterion as useful for distinguishing ethnic groups from "lower order collectivities that also use the vocabulary of kinship." The term "lower order" only makes sense from a modern perspective that imposes how local and national relate today onto the ancient Mediterranean.

Anatolian that all peoples of the peninsula shared. This possibility is at times assumed or addressed in partial ways, as discussed at the end of section one. But it is only by looking at the majority of its peoples that their quite distinct histories stand out.[387]

Acknowledgments

This work was especially made possible thanks to a Project Development Grant from the American Council of Learned Societies, as well as summer research funding from my home institution. I must also express deep appreciation to my lead editor, Denise Demetriou, for her invaluable feedback at various stages of composition, and her patience at my infelicitous oversights. Thanks also go to Denver Graninger and Matt Simonton, who commented on select sections in draft format, to Lee Brice, whose careful editorial eye caught many errors, and to the two anonymous reviewers, whose suggestions greatly improved the clarity and force of my arguments.

Bibliography

Adak, M. 2013. "Names, Ethnicity and Acculturation." In *Personal Names in Ancient Anatolia*, edited by R. Parker, 63–78. Oxford.

Adiego, I.J. 2007. *The Carian Language*. Leiden.

Adiego, I.J. 2013. "Carian Identity and Carian Language." In *4th-Century Karia: Defining a Karian Identity under the Hekatomnids*, edited by O. Henry, 15–20. Istanbul.

Adiego, I.J. 2019. "'Archaic' Carian." In *KARIA ARKHAIA: La Carie, des origines à la période pré-hékatomnide*, edited by O. Henry and K. Konuk, 23–42. Istanbul.

Akıncı Öztürk, E., and H. Malay. 2012. "Four Funerary Curses Recording the Pisidian Gods of the Acıpayam Plain." *EA* 45: 89–92.

Akurgal, E. 1993. "Die einheimische und fremden Elemente in der lykischen Kunst und ihre Eigenheiten." In *Akten des II. Internationalen Lykien-Symposions*, edited by J. Borchhardt and G. Dobesch, 149–59. Vienna.

Alkan, M. 2014. "Some Isaurian and Lycaonian Inscriptions in the Museum of Karaman." *Gephyra* 11: 51–63.

Alonso Troncoso, V. 2009. "The Hellenistic Gymnasium and the Pleasures of Paideia," *SPhP* 19: 71–84.

---

387   Cf. Greaves 2007, 2–4.

Andreeva, E. 2020. "Phrygian Inventions by Pliny the Elder." *Shagi/Steps* 6 (1): 57–72.
Arroyo Quirce, H. 2016. "Los orígines griegos de una ciudad de Pisidia: Selge, Esparta, y Calcante." *Emerita* 84 (1): 51–71.
Arroyo Quirce, H. 2020. "Greek Epic in Pisidia: The Solymi at Termessus." In *Greek Paideia and Local Tradition in the Graeco-Roman East*, edited by M.P. de Hoz, J. García Alonso, and L. Guichard Romero, 183–98. Leuven.
Ashton, R., and A. Meadows. 2008. "The Letoön Deposit: Lycian League Coinage, Rhodian Plinthophori, and Pseudo-Rhodian Drachms from Haliartos (yet again) and Asia Minor." *NC* 168: 111–34.
Aslan, N. 2011. "Eisenzeitliche Keramik aus Kilikien." In *Hellenismus in der Kilikia Pedias*, edited by A. Hoffmann, R. Posamentir, and M. Sayar, 1–17. Istanbul.
Attoura, H. 2002. "Aspekte der Akkulturation." In *Brückenland Anatolien? Ursachen, Extensität, und Modi des Kulturaustausches zwischen Anatolien und seinen Nachbarn*, edited by H. Blum et al., 19–33. Tübingen.
Aubriet, D. 2013. "Mylasa et l'identité carien." In *4th-Century Karia: Defining a Karian Identity under the Hekatomnids*, edited by O. Henry, 189–208. Istanbul.
Avram, A. 1984. "Bemerkungen zu den Mariandynern von Herakleia am Pontos." *StudClas* 22: 19–28.
Avram, A. 2013. "Indigenous Names in Heracleia Pontica." In *Personal Names in Ancient Anatolia*, edited by R. Parker, 51–62. Oxford.
Aytaçları, M. 2019. "The Geometric Pottery from Milas TKİ Excavations." In *KARIA ARKHAIA: La Carie, des origines à la période pré-hékatomnide*, edited by O. Henry and K. Konuk, 467–86. Istanbul.
Bachvarova, M. 2015. "Migrations in Anatolian Narrative Traditions." In *Nostoi: Indigenous Culture, Migration, and Integration in the Aegean Islands and Western Anatolia during the Bronze and Early Iron Ages*, edited by N. Stampolidis, Ç. Maner, and K. Kopanias, 145–83. Istanbul.
Baldriga, R. 1997. "Aspetti ideologici della presenza frigia nella tradizione greca sul regno di Lidia." In *Frigi e Frigio*, edited by R. Gusmani, M. Salvini, and P. Vannicelli, 279–85. Rome.
Ballesteros Pastor, L. 2006. "Influencia helénica y vida ciudadana en el reino del Ponto: La difícil búsqueda de una identidad." In *La construcción ideológica de la ciudadanía*, edited by D. Plácido et al., 381–94. Madrid.
Ballesteros Pastor, L. 2013. "*Nullis umquam nisi domesticis regibus*. Cappadocia, Pontus, and the Resistance to the Diadochi in Asia Minor." In *After Alexander: The Time of the Diadochi*, edited by V. Troncoso and E. Anson, 183–98. Oxford.
Ballesteros Pastor, L. 2016. "Comana Pontica in Hellenistic Times: A Cultural Crossroads." In *Between Tarhuntas and Zeus Polieus: Cultural Crossroads in the Temples and Cults of Graeco-Roman Anatolia*, edited by M.P. de Hoz et al., 47–73. Leuven.

Ballesteros Pastor, L. 2020. "Between Magian Lore and Greek *Paideia*: Royal Education in the Kingdom of Pontus." In *Greek* Paideia *and Local Tradition in the Graeco-Roman East*, edited by M.P. de Hoz, J. García Alonso, and L. Guichard Romero, 1–18. Leuven.

Baralis, A. 2015. "Le statut de la main d'oeuvre à Héraclée du Pont et en Mer Noire." In *La main d'oeuvre agricole en méditerranée archaïque: Status et dynamiques économiques*, edited by J. Zurbach, 197–234. Bordeaux.

Barat, C. 2013. "La Paphlagonie: Histoire et peuplement." In *L'Anatolie des peuples, des cités et des cultures (IIe millenaire av. J.C.–Ve siècle ap. J.C.)*. Vol. 1. *Autour d'un projet d'atlas historique et archéologique de l'Asie Mineure. Méthodologie et prospective*, edited by H. Bru and G. Labarre, 151–66. Franché-Compté.

Barnett, R. 1967. "Phrygia and the Peoples of Anatolia in the Iron Age." In *The Cambridge Ancient History*, Vol. 2. Part 2. *The Middle East and the Aegean Region, c. 1380–1000 BC*. 3rd ed., edited by I. Edwards et al., 417–442. Cambridge.

Baughan, E. 2010. "Lydian Burial Customs." In *The Lydians and Their World*, edited by N. Cahill, 273–304. Istanbul.

Beekes, R. 2002. "The Prehistory of the Lydians, the Origins of the Etruscans, Troy, and Aeneas." *BO* 54: 205–41.

Beekes, R. 2003. "Luwians and Lydians." *Kadmos* 42: 47–49.

Behrwald, R. 2000. *Der lykische Bund: Untersuchungen zu Geschichte und Verfassung*. Bonn.

Behrwald, R. 2015. "The Lykian League." In *Federalism in Greek Antiquity*, edited by H. Beck and P. Funke, 403–18. Cambridge.

Bellucci, E. 2000. "L'ottica regionale Di Strabone." In *Strabone e l'Asia Minore*, edited by D. Biraschi and G. Salmeri, 237–60. Naples.

Benda-Weber, I. 2005. *Lykier und Karer. Zwei autochtone ethnien Kleinasiens zwischen Orient und Okzident*. Bonn.

Bengisu, R. 1994. "Torrhebia Limne." *Arkeoloji Dergisi* 2: 33–43.

Berlin, A. 2019. "The Archaeology of a Changing City." In *Spear-Won Land: Sardis from the King's Peace to the Peace of Apamea*, edited by A. Berlin and P. Kosmin, 50–67. Madison.

Berlin, A., and P. Kosmin. 2019. *Spear-Won Land: Sardis from the King's Peace to the Peace of Apamea*. Madison.

Berndt-Ersöz, S. 2006. *Phrygian Rock-Cut Shrines: Structure, Function, and Cult Practice*. Leiden.

Bhabha, H. 1994. *The Location of Culture*. New York.

Bielfeldt, R. 2019. "Pergamum and Sardis: Models of Neighborliness." In *Spear-Won Land: Sardis from the King's Peace to the Peace of Apamea*, edited by A. Berlin and P. Kosmin, 167–90. Madison.

Billows, R. 1995. *Kings and Colonists: Aspects of Macedonian Imperialism*. Leiden.

Bing, J. 1968. *A History of Cilicia during the Assyrian Period*. Ann Arbor.

Blum, H. 2002. "Überlegungen zum Thema 'Akkulturation.'" In *Brückenland Anatolien? Ursachen, Extensität, und Modi des Kulturaustausches zwischen Anatolien und seinen Nachbarn*, edited by H. Blum, B. Faist, P. Pfälzner, and A.-M. Wittke, 1–17. Tübingen.

Blümel, W. 1992. "Einheimische Personennamen in griechischen Inschriften aus Karien." *EA* 20: 7–33.

Blümel, W. 2009. "Zur Schrift und Sprach der Karer." In *Die Karer und die Anderen*, edited by F. Rumscheid, 221–27. Bonn.

Bøgh, B. 2007. "The Phrygian Background of Kybele." *Numen* 54.3: 304–39.

Bokisch, G., P. Ruggendorfer, and L. Zabrana. 2013. "Temple and Altars for Greek and Carian Gods: New Evidence for Religious Life in Alinda during the Late Classical and Hellenistic Period." In *4th-Century Karia: Defining a Karian Identity under the Hekatomnids*, edited by O. Henry, 129–62. Istanbul.

Bonnet, C. 2015. *Les enfants de Cadmos: Le paysage religieux de la Phénicie hellénistique*. Paris.

Bonnet, C. 2019. "The Hellenistic Period and Hellenization in Phoenicia." In *The Oxford Handbook of the Phoenician and Punic Mediterranean*, edited by C. López-Ruiz and B. Doak, 99–110. Oxford.

Borchhardt, J. 2003. "Lykische Inschriften im archäologischen kontext." In *Licia e Lidia prima dell'ellenizzazione*, edited by M. Giorgieri et al., 37–67. Rome.

Bousquet, J. 1975. "Arbinas, fils de Gergis, dynaste de Xanthos." *CRAI* 10: 138–48.

Bousquet, J. 1992a. "Les inscriptions du Létôon en l'honneur d'Arbinas et l'epigramme grecque de la stèle de Xanthos." In *Fouilles de Xanthos*, 9.1, edited by P. Klinck and H. Metzger: 155–88. Paris.

Bousquet, J. 1992b. "L'inscription bilingue de Démocleidès et les inscriptions lyciennes unilingues." In *Fouilles de Xanthos*, 9.1, edited by P. Klinck and H. Metzger: 189–96. Paris.

Boyxen, B. 2018. *Fremde in der hellenistischen Polis Rhodos*. Berlin.

Bremen, R. van. 2000. "The demes and phylai of Stratonikeia in Karia." *Chiron* 30: 389–401.

Bremen, R. van. 2004. "Leon son of Chrysaor and the Religious Identity of Stratonikeia in Caria." In *The Greco-Roman East: Politics, Culture, Society*, edited by S. Colvin, 207–44. Cambridge.

Bremmer, J. 2009. "Zeus' Own Country: Cult and Myth in the Pride of Halicarnassus." In *Antiken Mythen: Medien, Transformationen und Konstruktionen*, edited by U. Dill and C. Walde, 292–312. Berlin.

Bremmer, J. 2013. "Local Mythography: The Pride of Halicarnassus." In *Writing Myth: Mythography in the Ancient World*, edited by S. Trzaskoma and R. Smith, 55–73. Leuven.

Bresson, A. 2001. "Grecs et Cariens dans la Chersonèse de Rhodes." In *Origines Gentium*, edited by V. Fromentin and S. Gotteland, 147–60. Pessac.

Bresson, A. 2007a. "Les Cariens ou la mauvaise conscience du barbare." In *Tra Oriente e Occidente. Indigeni, greci e romani in Asia Minore*, edited by G. Urso, 209–28. Pisa.

Bresson, A. 2007b. "Unity, Diversity, and Conflict in Hellenistic Lycia." In *Regionalism in Hellenistic and Roman Asia Minor*, edited by H. Elton and G. Reger, 73–79. Bordeaux.

Bresson, A. 2009. "Karien und die dorische Kolonisation." In *Die Karer und die Anderen*, edited by F. Rumscheid, 109–20. Bonn.

Briant, P. 1985. "Dons de terres et de villes: L'Asie Mineure dans le context achémenide." *REA* 87 (1–2): 53–72.

Briant, P. 2002. *From Cyrus to Alexander a History of the Persian Empire*, edited by Peter T. Daniels. Winona Lake, IN.

Briant, P. 2006. "L'Asie Mineure en transition." In *La transition entre l'empire achéménide et les royaumes hellénistique (vers 350–300 av. J.C.)*, edited by P. Briant and F. Joannés, 309–51. Paris.

Bringmann, K. 2004. "Gymnasion und griechische Bildung im Nahen Osten." In *Das hellenistische Gymnasion*, edited by D. Kah and P. Scholz, 323–33. Berlin.

Brixhe, C. 1993. "Le grec en Carie et en Lycie au IVe siècle." In *La koiné grecque antique*, edited by C. Brixhe, 59–82. Nancy.

Brixhe, C. 2007. "The Phrygians and the Phrygian Language." In *The Mysterious Civilization of the Phrygians*, edited by S. Şentürk, 148–60. Istanbul.

Brixhe, C. 2012. "Phrygian Language (through Prehistory and History)." In *Phrygians: In the Land of Midas, in the Shadow of Monuments*, edited by T. Sivas and H. Sivas, 234–41. Istanbul.

Brixhe, C. 2013a. "Anatolian Anthroponymy after Louis Robert ... and Some Others." In *Personal Names in Ancient Anatolia*, edited by R. Parker, 15–30. Oxford.

Brixhe, C. 2013b. "The Personal Onomastics of Roman Phrygia." In *Roman Phrygia: Culture and Society*, edited by P. Thonemann, 55–69. Cambridge.

Brixhe, C. 2016a. "Au long de l'Eurymédon: Le pisidien." *Res Antiquae* 2016: 29–36.

Brixhe, C. 2016b. *Stèles et langue de Pisidie*. Nancy.

Brixhe, C., and R. Tekoğlu. 2000. "Corpus des inscriptions dialectales de Pamphylie: Supplément 5." *Kadmos* 39: 1–56.

Brock, R. 1996. "Thucydides and the Athenian Purification of Delos." *Mnemosyne* 49.3: 321–27.

Bru, H. 2017. *La Phrygie Parorée et la Pisidie septentrionale aux époques hellénistique et romaine: Géographique historique et sociologie culturelle*. Leiden.

Bru, H., A. Dumitru, and N. Sekunda. 2021. "Introduction." In *Colonial Geopolitics and Local Cultures in the Hellenistic and Roman East (3rd Century BCE–3rd Century AD)*, edited by H. Bru, A. Dumitru, and N. Sekunda, 1–5. Oxford.

Brun, P. 2007. "La Carie et les cariens vus depuis Athènes a l'époque classique." In *Scripta Anatolica*, edited by P. Brun, 15–32. Bordeaux.
Bryce, T. 1986. *The Lycians in Literary and Epigraphic Sources*. Copenhagen.
Bryce, T. 1990. "Hellenism in Lycia." In *Greek Colonists and Native Populations*, edited by J.-P. Descoeudres, 531–41. Oxford.
Bryce, T. 2016. "The Land of Hiyawa (Que) Revisited." *AS* 66: 67–79.
Burgess, W. 1990. "Isaurian Names and the Ethnic Identity of the Isaurians in Late Antiquity." *AncW* 21: 109–21.
Burkert, W. 1995. "Lydia between East and West or How to Date the Trojan War: A Study in Herodotus." In *The Ages of Homer*, edited by J. Carter and S. Morris, 139–48. Austin.
Burney, C., and D. 1971. *The Peoples of the Hills: Ancient Ararat and Caucasus*. New Haven.
Burstein, S. 1976. *Outpost of Hellenism: The Emergence of Heraclea on the Black Sea*. Berkeley.
Cahill, N. 2019. "Inside Out: Sardis in the Achaemenid and Lysimachean Periods." In *Spear-Won Land: Sardis from the King's Peace to the Peace of Apamea*, edited by A. Berlin and P. Kosmin, 11–36. Madison.
Capdetrey, L. 2007. *Le pouvoir séleucide: Territoire, administration, finances d'un royaume hellénistique (312–129 Av. J.-C.)*. Rennes.
Capdetrey, L. 2012. "Le roi, le satrape et le koinon." In *Stephanèphoros. De l'économie antique à l'Asie Mineure*, edited by K. Konuk and R. Descat, 229–46. Pessac.
Carpenter, J. and D. Boyd. 1977. "Dragon Houses. Euboia, Attika, Karia." *AJA* 81: 179–215.
Carruba, O. 1996. "Appendice Lessicale." In *Monetazione arcaica della lycia III: Le primi emissioni di Wedri*, edited by N. Vismara, 211–19. Milan.
Carruba, O. 2003. "Λυδικὴ Ἀρχαιολογία. La Lidia fra II et I millennio." In *Licia e Lidia prima dell'ellenizzazione*, edited by M. Giorgieri et al., 145–67. Rome.
Carstens, A.-M. 2002. "Tomb and Cult on the Halikarnassos Peninsula." *AJA* 106: 391–409.
Carstens, A.-M. 2009. *Karia and the Hekatomnids: The Creation of a Dynasty*. Oxford.
Casabonne, O. 2001. "De Tarse à Mazaka et de Tarkumuwa à Datames: D'une Cilicie à l'autre?" In *La Cilicie: Éspaces et pouvoirs locaux*, edited by E. Jean, A. Dinçol, and S. Durugönül, 243–61. Paris.
Casabonne, O. 2004. *La Cilicie à l'époque achémenide*. Paris.
Chaniotis, A. 2009. "Myths and Contexts in Aphrodisias." In *Antiken Mythen: Medien, Transformationen und Konstruktionen*, edited by U. Dill and C. Walde, 313–38. Berlin.
Chrubasik, B. 2017. "From Pre-Makkabaean Judaea to Hekatamnid Karia and Back Again: The Question of Hellenization." In *Hellenism and the Local Communities of the Eastern Mediterranean. 400BCE–250CE*, edited by B. Chrubasik and D. King, 83–109. Oxford.

Chrubasik, B., and D. King. 2017. "Hellenism? An Introduction." In *Hellenism and the Local Communities of the Eastern Mediterranean. 400BCE–250CE*, edited by B. Chrubasik and D. King, 1–11. Oxford.

Cohen, G. 1995. *The Hellenistic Settlements in Europe, the Islands, and Asia Minor*. Berkeley.

Coles-Rannous, F. 2013. "Circulation et production d'images: Autour de la question de l'identité lycienne." In *Euploia. La Lycie et la Carie antiques. Dynamiques des territoires, échanges et identités*, edited by P. Brun et al., 51–60. Bordeaux.

Colvin, S. 2004. "Names in Hellenistic and Roman Lycia." In *The Greco-Roman East: Politics, Culture, Society*, edited by S. Colvin, 44–84. Cambridge.

Connor, W. 1994. *Ethno-nationalism: The Quest for Understanding*. Princeton.

Constantakopoulou, C. 2017. *Aegean Interactions: Delos and its Networks in the Third Century*. Oxford.

Corsaro, M. 1984. "Un decreto di Zeleia sul recupero dei terreni publici (*Syll.*³ 279)." *ASNP* 14 (2): 441–93.

Corsten, T. 2007. "Thracian Personal Names and Military Settlements in Hellenistic Bithynia." In *Old and New Worlds in Greek Onomastics*, edited by E. Matthews, 121–33. Oxford.

Coulton, J.J. 1993. "North Lycia before the Romans." In *Akten des II. Internationalen Lykien-Symposions*, edited by J. Borchhardt and G. Dobesch, 79–85. Vienna.

Courtils, J. des. 2001. "L'archéologie du peuple lycien." In *Origines Gentium*, edited by V. Fromentin and S. Gotteland, 123–33. Bordeaux.

Cox, C., and A. Cameron. 1932. "A Native Inscription from the Myso-Phrygian Borderland." *Klio* 25: 34–49.

Crielaard, J. 2009. "The Ionians in the Archaic Period: Shifting Identities in a Changing World." In *Ethnic Constructs in Antiquity: The Role of Power and Tradition*, edited by T. Terks and N. Roymans, 37–84. Amsterdam.

Curty, O. 1995. *Les parentés légendaires entre cités grecques: Catalogue raisonné des inscriptions contenant le terme syngeneia et analyse critique*. Geneva.

D'Alessio, G.B. 2004. "Some Notes on the Salmakis Inscription." In *The Salmakis Inscription and Hellenistic Harlicarnassos*, edited by S. Isager and P. Pedersen, 43–57. Odense.

Dan, A. 2010. "Les Leukosyriens: Quelques notes d'ethnographie sinopéenne." *Ancient Civilizations from Scythia to Siberia* 16: 73–102.

Dana, D. 2016. "Onomastique indigène à Byzance et à Cyzique." In *Identité régionale, identités civiques autour des détroits des Dardanelles et du Bosphore*, edited by M. Dana and F. Prêteux, 47–68. Franché-Compté.

Dana, M. 2016. "Histoire et historiens de Propontide et de Bithynie: Mythes, récits, et identités." In *Identité régionale, identités civiques autour des détroits des Dardanelles et du Bosphore*, edited by M. Dana and F. Prêteux, 171–240. Franché-Compté.

Dana, M. 2020. "Local Culture and Regional Cultures in Propontis and Bithynia." In *Greek Paideia and Local Tradition in the Graeco-Roman East*, edited by M.-P. de Hoz, J. García Alonso, and L. Guichard Romero, 39–71. Leuven.

Daubner, F. 2015. "*Gymnasia*: Aspects of a Greek Institution in the Hellenistic and Roman Near East." In *Religious Identities in the Levant from Alexander to Muhammad*, edited by M. Blömer, A. Lichtenberger, and R. Raja, 33–46. Turnhout.

Debord, P. 1985. "La Lydie du nord-est." *REA* 87: 345–58.

Debord, P. 1994. "Essai sur la geographie historique de la region de Stratonicée." In *Mélanges Pierre Lévêque, 8. Religion, Anthropologie et Société*, edited by M. Mactoux and É. Geny, 107–21. Paris.

Debord, P. 2001. "Les Mysiens: Du mythe à l'histoire." In *Origines Gentium*, edited by V. Fromentin and S. Gotteland, 135–46. Bordeaux.

Debord, P. 2003. "Cité grecque – village carien." *Studi ellenistici* 15: 115–80.

Debord, P. 2005. "Côte/Intérieur: Les acculturations de la Carie." *PP* 60: 357–78.

Debord, P. 2009. "Peut-on définir un panthéon carien?" In *Die Karer und die anderen*, edited by F. Rumscheid, 251–65. Bonn.

Debord, P. 2013. "Hécate, divinité carienne." In *Euploia. La Lycie et la Carie antiques. Dynamiques des territoires, échanges et identités*, edited by P. Brun et al., 85–91. Bordeaux.

Demargne, P. 1974. "Xanthos et les problèmes de l'hellénisation au temps de la Grèce classique." *CRAI* 118 (4): 584–90.

Desideri, P. 1991. "Cilicia ellenistica. Scambi ed identitá culturale." In *Scambi e identitá culturale: La Cilicia*, edited by P. Desideri and S. Settis, 141–65. Bologna.

Devijver, H. 1996. "Local Elite, Equestrians and Senators in the Social History of Roman Sagalassos." *AncSoc* 27: 105–62.

Diakonoff, I., and V. Neroznak. 1985. *Phrygian*. Delmar, NY.

Dietler, M. 2010. *Archaeologies of Colonialism: Consumption, Entanglement, and Violence in Ancient Mediterranean France*. Berkeley.

Dignas, B. 2012. "Rituals and the Construction of Identity in Attalid Pergamon." In *Historical and Religious Memory in the Ancient World*, edited by B. Dignas and R. Smith, 119–44. Oxford.

Domingo Gygax, M. 2001. *Untersuchungen zu den lykischen Gemeinwesen in klassischer und hellenistischer Zeit*. Bonn.

Dongen, E. van. 2014. "The Extent and Interactions of the Phrygian Kingdom." In *From Source to History: Studies on Ancient Near Eastern Worlds and Beyond*, edited by S. Gaspa et al., 697–711. Münster.

Doni, C. 2009. "The Pisidians: From Their Origin to Their Western Expansion." In *L'Asie Mineure dans l'antiquité: Échanges, populations et territoires*, edited by H. Bru, F. Kirbihler, and S. Lebreton, 213–27. Rennes.

Drew-Bear, T., and G. Labarre. 2004. "Un dédicace aux 12 dieux lyciens et la question de leur origine." In *Les cultes locaux dans les mondes grec et romain*, edited by G. Labarre, 81–101. Lyon.

Drews, R. 1993. "Myths of Midas and the Phrygian Migration from Europe." *Klio* 75: 9–26.

Dusinberre, E. 2013. *Empire, Authority, and Autonomy in Achaemenid Anatolia*. Oxford.

Dusinberre, E. 2019. "Sealstones from Sardis, Dascylium, and Gordion." In *Spear-Won Land: Sardis from the King's Peace to the Peace of Apamea*, edited by A. Berlin and P. Kosmin, 37–43. Madison.

Eckhardt, B. 2016. "Romanisation and Isomorphic Change in Phrygia: The Case of Private Associations." *JRS* 106: 147–71.

Eichner, H. 2016. "Die Identität der Lyker im Licht ihres gespalten Ethnonyms." In *Angekommen auf Ithaka. Festgabe für Jürgen Borchhardt zum 80. Geburtstag*, edited by F. Blakolmer, M. Seyer, and H.D. Szemethy, 59–66. Vienna.

Ellis-Evans, A. 2019. *The Kingdom of Priam: Lesbos and the Troad between Anatolia and the Aegean*. Oxford.

Elton, H. 2007. "Geography, Labels, Romans, and Kilikia." In *Regionalism in Hellenistic and Roman Asia Minor*, edited by H. Elton and G. Reger, 25–31. Bordeaux.

Engels, D. 2017. "The Achaemenid and Seleucid Court: Continuity or Change?" In *The Hellenistic Court: Monarchic Power and Elite Society from Alexander to Cleopatra*, edited by A. Erskine, L. Llewellyn-Jones, and S. Wallace, 69–100. Swansea.

Erskine, A. 2005. "Unity and Identity: Shaping the Past in the Greek Mediterranean." In *Cultural Borrowings and Ethnic Appropriations in Antiquity*, edited by E. Gruen, 121–36. Stuttgart.

Fabiani, R. 2000. "Strabone e la Caria." In *Strabone e l'Asia Minore*, edited by A. Biraschi and G. Salmeri, 373–400. Naples.

Faraguna, M. 1995. "Note di storia milesia arcaica: I Γέργιθες e la στάσις di VI secolo." *SMEA* 36: 37–89.

Fernoux, H.-L. 2004. *Notables et élites des cités de Bithynie aux époques hellénistique et romaine*. Lyon.

Fernoux, H.-L. 2013. "Bithyniens et grecs d'Asie: À propos de la notion d'identité provinciale en Asie Mineure sous le haut empire." In *Identités et dynamiques provinciales du IIe siècle avant notre ère à l'époque julio-claudienne*, edited by S. Lefebvre, 61–88. Dijon.

Ferrary, J.-L. 2001. "Rome et la géographie de l'hellénisme: Réflexions sur 'hellènes' et 'Panhellènes' dans les inscriptions d'époque romaine." In *The Greek East in the Roman Context*, edited by O. Salomies, 19–35. Helsinki.

Ferrary, J.-L. 2011. "La géographie de l'hellénisme sous la domination romaine." *Phoenix* 65 (1–2): 1–22.

Flaig, E. 1999. "Über die Grenzen der Akkulturation: Wider die Verdinglichung des Kulturbegriffs." In *Reception und Identität: Die kulturelle Auseinandersetzung Roms mit Griechenland als europäisches Paradigma*, edited by G. Vogt-Spira, B. Rommell, and I. Müsaus, 81–112. Stuttgart.

Fontaine, E. 2018. "Hérodote et les lydiens: Histoire d'une errance." *LEC* 86: 125–36.

Fontrier, A. 1896. "Funde." *MDAI(A)* 21: 375–76.

Forlanini, M. 2003. "I gruppi linguistici nell'Anatolia occidentale e il problema dell'etnogenesi Lidia. Alcuni indizi?" In *Licia e Lidia prima dell'ellenizzazione*, edited by M. Giorgieri et al., 171–86. Rome.

Forlanini, M. 2013. "La survie des toponyms de l'âge du Bronze dans le Pont et en Cappadoce. Continuité ethnique, linguistique, et survie des traditions de l'époque hittite impériale pendant les siècles 'obscurs' jusqu'au début de l'âge classique?" In *L'Anatolie des peuples, des cités et des cultures (IIe millenaire av. J.C.–Ve siècle ap. J.C.). Vol. 1. Autour d'un projet d'atlas historique et archéologique de l'Asie Mineure. Méthodologie et prospective*, edited by H. Bru and G. Labarre, 69–84. Franché-Compté.

Franck, L. 1966. "Sources classiques concernant la Cappadoce." *Revue hittite et asianique* 24: 5–122.

Fraser, P., and E. Matthews. 2010. *A Lexicon of Greek Personal Names*. Vol. 5A. *Coastal Asia Minor: Pontos to Ionia*. Oxford.

Frei, P. 1990. "Die Götterkulte Lykiens in der Kaiserheit." In *Aufstieg und Niedergang der römischen Welt* II.18.3, edited by H. Temporini and W. Haase, 1730–1864. Berlin.

Frei, P. 1993. "Solymer-Milyer-Termilen-Lykier: Ethnische und politische Einheiten auf eher lykischen Halbinsel." In *Akten des II. Internationalen Lykien-Symposions*, edited by J. Borchhardt and G. Dobesch, 87–97. Vienna.

Frézouls, E. 1991. "L'hellénisme dans l'épigraphie de l'Asie Mineure." In *Ελληνισμός. Quelques jalons pour une histoire de l'identité grecque*, edited by S. Said, 125–47. Leiden.

Gabelko, O. 2017. "Bithynia and Cappadocia: Royal Courts and Ruling Society in the Minor Hellenistic Monarchies." In *The Hellenistic Court: Monarchic Power and Elite Society from Alexander to Cleopatra*, edited by A. Erskine, L. Llewelyn-Jones, and S. Wallace, 319–42. Swansea.

Gabrielsen, V. 2011. "The Chrysaoreis of Caria." In *Labraunda and Karia. Proceedings of the International Symposium Commemorating Sixty Years of Swedish Archaeological Work in Labraunda*, edited by L. Karlsson and S. Carlsson, 331–53. Uppsala.

Gagné, R. 2006. "What Is the Pride of Halicarnassus?" *ClAnt* 25.1: 1–33.

Gallotta, S. 2005. "Tra integrazione ed emarginazione: Gli indigeni nelle *poleis* greche del Mar Nero." In *Serta antiqua et mediaevalia. 7: Il cittadino, lo straniero, il barbaro fra integrazione ed emarginazione nell'antichità: Atti del I incontro internazionale di storia antica: (Genova 22–24 Maggio 2003)*, edited by A. Bertinelli, M. Gabriella, and A. Donati, 427–36. Rome.

Gander, M. 2012. "Ahhiyawa-Hiyawa-Que: Gibt es Evidenz für die Anwesenheit von Griechen in Kilikia am Übergang der Bronze- zur Eisenzeit," *SMEA* 54: 281–309.

Gander, M. 2016. "Lukka, Lycians, Trmmili in Ancient Near Eastern Sources." In *Lukka'dan Likya'ya: Sarpedon ve Aziz Nikolaos'un Ülkesi/From Lukka to Lycia: The Land of Sarpedon and Saint Nicholas*, edited by H. İşkan and E. Dündar, 80–99. Istanbul.

Gatzke, A. 2019. "Mithridates VI Eupator and Persian Kingship." *AHB* 33.1–2: 60–80.

Gauthier, P. 1989. *Nouvelles inscriptions de Sardis. II*. Geneva.

Genz, H. 2011. "The Iron Age in Central Anatolia." In *The Black Sea, Greece, Anatolia, and Europe in the First Millennium BC*, edited by G. Tsetskhladze and J. Bouzek, 331–68. Leuven.

Goedegebuure, P. et al. 2020. "Türkmen-Karahöyük 1: A New Hieroglyphic Luwian Inscription from Great King Hartapu, son of Mursili, conqueror of Phrygia." *AS* 70: 29–43.

Gorman, B. 2009. "The Invention of Marriage: Hermaphroditus and Salmacis at Halicarnassus and in Ovid." *CQ* 59: 543–61.

Grainger, J. 2009. *The Cities of Pamphylia*. Oxford.

Greaves, A. 2007. "Trans-Anatolia: Examining Turkey as a Bridge between East and West." *Anatolian* 57: 1–15.

Greaves, A. 2019. "'Greek' Colonization: The View from Ionia." In *Greek Colonization in Local Contexts*, edited by J. Lucas, A. Murray, and S. Owen, 231–41. Cambridge.

Groß-Albenhausen, K. 2004. "Bedeutung und Funktion der Gymnasien für die Hellenisierung des Ostens." In *Das hellenistische Gymnasion*, edited by D. Kah and P. Scholz, 71–81. Berlin.

Gruen, E. 2000. "Culture as Policy: The Attalids of Pergamon." In *From Pergamon to Sperlonga: Sculpture and Context*, edited by N. De Grummond and B. Ridgeway, 17–31. Berkeley.

Gruen, E. 2020. *Ethnicity in the Ancient World: Did It Matter?* Berlin.

Gusmani, R. et al. 2002. "TITUS: Corpus of Lydian Inscriptions." 2002. http://titus.uni-frankfurt.de/texte/etcs/anatol/lydian/lydcot.htm.

Haider, P. 2008. "War ein Groß-Ionien tatsächlich um 1360 v. Chr. in Westkleinasien existent? Eine kritische Analyse zu den Lesungen und Identifizierungen der jüngst entdeckten topographischen Namenlisten aus der Regierungszeit Amenophis' III." *Klio* 90.2: 291–306.

Hall, A. 1986. "Regional Epigraphic Catalogues of Asia Minor, Notes and Studies, IX: The Milyadeis and their Territory." *AS* 36: 137–57.

Hall, A., and J. Coulton. 1990. "A Hellenistic Allotment List from Balboura in the Kibyratis." *Chiron* 20: 109–55.

Hall, E. 1989. *Inventing the Barbarian: Greek Self-Definition Through Tragedy*. Oxford.

Hall, J. 1997. *Ethnic Identity in Greek Antiquity*. Cambridge.

Hall, J. 2002. *Hellenicity: Between Ethnicity and Culture*. Chicago.

Hall, J. 2015. "Ancient Greek Ethnicities: Toward a Reassessment." *BICS* 58: 15–29.

Hannestad, L. 1996. "'This Contributes in No Small Way to One's Reputation': The Bithynian Kings and Greek Culture." In *Aspects of Hellenistic Kingship*, edited by P. Bilde et al., 67–98. Aarhus.

Hansen, E. 1971. *The Attalids of Pergamon*. 2nd ed. Ithaca.

Hansen, E., and C. Le Roy. 1976. "Au Létôon de Xanthos: Les deux temples de Léto." *RA*: 317–36.

Hansen, E. 2012. *Fouilles de Xanthos. 11. Le Temple de Léto au Létôon de Xanthos: Étude Architecturale*. Aarhus.

Hansen, M.H., and T.H. Nielsen. 2004. *An Inventory of Archaic and Classical Poleis*. Oxford.

Harrison, T. 2019. "Classical Greek Ethnography and the Slave Trade." *Classical Antiquity* 38 (1): 36–57.

Haubold, J. 2013. *Greece and Mesopotamia: Dialogues in Literature*. Cambridge.

Hawkins, J. 2000. *Corpus of Hieroglyphic Luwian Inscriptions. Vol. 1. Inscriptions of the Iron Age*. Berlin.

Held, W. 2009. "Die Karer und die rhodische Peraia." In *Die Karer und die Anderen*, edited by F. Rumscheid, 121–34. Bonn.

Heller, A. 2006. *Les bêtises des grecs*. Bordeaux.

Heller, A. 2009. "Généalogies locales et construction des identités collectives en Asie Mineure." In *L'Asie Mineure dans l'antiquité: Échanges, populations et territoires*, edited by H. Bru, F. Kirbihler, and S. Lebreton, 53–65. Rennes.

Hellström, P. 2009. "Sacred Architecture and Karian Identity." In *Die Karer und die Anderen*, edited by F. Rumscheid, 267–90. Bonn.

Hemer, C. 1980. "The Pisidian Texts: A Problem of Language and History." *Kadmos* 19.1: 54–64.

Henkelman, W. and M. Stolper. 2009. "Ethnic Identity and Ethnic Labelling at Persepolis: The case of the Skudrians." In *Organisation des pouvoirs et contacts culturels dans le pays de l'empire achéménide*, edited by P. Briant and M. Chauveau, 271–328. Paris.

Henry, O. 2010. "Hektamnos, Persian Satrap or Greek Dynast? The Tomb at Berber İni." In *Hellenistic Karia*, edited by R. van Bremen and J.-M. Carbon, 103–22. Bordeaux.

Henry, O. 2013a. "Introduction." In *4th-Century Karia: Defining a Karian Identity under the Hekatomnids*, edited by O. Henry, 5–8. Istanbul.

Henry, O. 2013b. "A Tribute to the Ionian Renaissance." In *4th-Century Karia: Defining a Karian Identity under the Hekatomnids*, edited by O. Henry, 81–90. Istanbul.

Herda, A. 2009. "Karkisa-Karien und die sogenannte ionische Migration." In *Die Karer und die Anderen*, edited by F. Rumscheid, 27–108. Bonn.

Herda, A. 2013. "Greek (and Our) Views on Karians." In *Luwian Identities*, edited by A. Mouton, I. Rutherford, and I. Yakubovitch, 421–506. Leiden.

Herda, A., and M. Sauter. 2009. "Karerinnen und Karer in Milet: Zu einem spätkarischen Schüsselchen mit karischem Graffito aus Milet." *AA*: 51–112.

Hoff, C. 2017. *Identität und Politik: Kollektive Kulturelle und politische Identität der Lykier bis zur Mitte des 4. Jahrhunderts v.Chr*. Wiesbaden.

Hönigmann, P., and N. Oettinger. 2018. *Lydien: Ein altanatolischer Staat zwischen Griechenland und dem Vorderen Orient*. Berlin.

Hornblower, S. 1982. *Mausolus*. Oxford.

Houwink ten Cate, P. 1965. *The Luwian Population Groups of Lycia and Cilicia Aspera during the Hellenistic Period*. Leiden.

Hovannisian, R. 1997. *The Armenian People from Ancient to Modern Times*. Vol. 1. *The Dynastic Periods: From Antiquity to the Fourteenth Century*. New York.

Hoz, M.P. de. 1999. *Die lydische Kulte im Lichte der griechischen Inschriften*. Bonn.

Hoz, M.P. de. 2005. "Los Solymoi: Identidad, pervivencia y relación con Licios, Milyai, y Kabaleis." *Geographica Antiqua* 14–15: 77–88.

Hoz, M.P. de. 2016. "The Goddess of Sardis: Artemis, Demeter, or Kore?" In *Between Tarhuntas and Zeus Polieus: Cultural Crossroads in the Temples and Cults of Graeco-Roman Anatolia*, edited by M. Paz de Hoz, J.P. Sanchez Hernández, and C. Molina Vintero, 185–221. Leuven.

Hutter, M. 2006. "Die phrygische Religion als Teil der Religionsgeschichte Anatoliens." In *Pluralismus und Wandel in den Religionen im vorhellenistichen Anatolien*, edited by M. Hutter and S. Hutter-Braunsar, 79–95. Münster.

Huxley, G. 1964. "Studies in Early Greek Poets." *GRBS* 5: 21–33.

Innocente, L. 1995. "Stato degli studi frigi." In *Atti del II congresso internazionale di hittitologia*, edited by O. Carruba, M. Giorgieri, and C. Mora, 213–24. Pavia.

İplikçioğlu, B., G. Çelgin and A. Çelgin. 2007. *Epigraphische Forschungen in Termessos und seinem Territorium IV*. Vienna.

Isager, S. 1998. "The Pride of Halicarnassos: Editio Princeps of an Inscription from Salmakis." *ZPE* 123: 1–23.

Isager, S. 2004. "The Salmakis Inscription: Some Reactions to the Editio Princeps." In *The Salmakis Inscription and Hellenistic Harlicarnassos*, edited by S. Isager and P. Pedersen, 9–13. Odense.

Işık, F. 2009. "Anadolu-İon Uygarlığı. 'Kolonizasyon' ve 'Doğu Hellen' Kavramlarına Eleştirel Bir Bakış." *Anadolu* 35: 53–86.

Işık, F. 2010. "Anadolu-Likya Uygarlığı. Likya'nın 'Hellenleşmesi' Görüşüne Eleştirel Bir Yaklaşım." *Anadolu* 36: 65–125.

Işık, F. 2012. *Uygarlık Anadoluda Doğdu*. Istanbul.

Işık, F. 2016. "On the Anatolian-Ionian Essence of the Lycian Civilization: In the case of Xanthos in the Dynastic Period." In *Lukka'dan Likya'ya: Sarpedon ve Aziz Nikolaos'un Ülkesi/From Lukka to Lycia: The Land of Sarpedon and Saint Nicholas*, edited by H. İşkan and E. Dündar, 436–59. Istanbul.

Jackson, C. 2017. "Dio Chrysostom." In *The Oxford Handbook of the Second Sophistic*, edited by D. Richter and W. Johnson, 217–32. Oxford.

Jasink, A., and L. Bombardieri. 2013. "The Göksu River Valley from the Late Bronze Age to Iron Age: Local Cultures, External Influences, and Relations with Foreign Peoples." In *Rough Cilicia: New Historical and Archaeological Approaches*, edited by M. Hoff and R. Townsend, 16–26. Oxford.

Jasink, A., and M. Marino. 2007. "The West Anatolian Origins of the Que Kingdom Dynasty." *SMEA* 49: 407–26.

Jenkins, F. 2016. "Menekrates of Xanthus (769)." In *Brill's New Jacoby*, edited by I. Worthington. http://dx.doi.org/10.1163/1873-5363_bnj_a769.

Jones, C.P. 1999. *Kinship Diplomacy in the Ancient World*. Cambridge.

Jonnes, L., and M. Ricl. 1997. "A New Royal Inscription from Phrygia Paroreios." *EA* 29: 1–30.

Karlsson, L. 2013. "Combining Architectural Orders at Labraunda." In *4th-Century Karia: Defining a Karian Identity under the Hekatomnids*, edited by O. Henry, 65–80. Istanbul.

Kearsley, R. 1994. "The City of Milyas and the Attalids: A Decree of the City of Olbasa and a New Royal Letter of the Second Century B.C." *AS* 44: 47–57.

Keen, A. 1998. *Dynastic Lycia*. Leiden.

Keil, J., and A. von Premerstein. 1914. *Bericht über eine dritte Reise in Lydien*. Vienna.

Kelp, U. 2013. "Grave Monuments and Local Identities in Roman Phrygia." In *Roman Phrygia: Culture and Society*, edited by P. Thonemann, 70–94. Cambridge.

Kelp, U. 2015. *Grabdenkmal und lokale Identität*. Bonn.

Kerschner, E. 2010. "The Lydians and Their Ionian and Aeolian Neighbors." In *The Lydians and Their World*, edited by N. Cahill, 247–65. Istanbul.

Klinkott, H. 2002. "Zur politische Akkulturation unter den Achaimeniden. Der Testfall Karien." In *Brückenland Anatolien? Ursachen, Extensität, und Modi des Kulturaustausches zwischen Anatolien und seinen Nachbarn*, edited by H. Blum et al., 173–204. Tübingen.

Klinkott, H. 2009. "Die Karer im Achaimenidenreich." In *Die Karer und die Anderen*, edited by F. Rumscheid, 149–62. Bonn.

Kolb, F. 2003. "Aspekte der Akkulturation in Zentrallykien in archaischer und klassischer Zeit." In *Licia e Lidia prima dell'ellenizzazione*, edited by M. Giorgieri et al., 207–38. Rome.

Kolb, F. 2007. "Akkulturation in der lykischen 'Provinz' unter römischer Herrshaft." In *Tra Oriente e Occidente. Indigeni, greci e romani in Asia Minore*, edited by G. Urso, 271–91. Pisa.

Kolb, F. 2014. "Lykien, Lykier, Termilen in der frühen griechischen Literatur: Ihr Beitrag zu griechischem Mythos und Historie." In *Der Beitrag Kleinasiens zur Kultur- und Geistesgeschichte der griechisch-römischen Antike*, edited by J. Fischer, 257–77. Vienna.

Kolb, F. 2018. *Lykien: Geschichte einer antiken Landschaft.* Darmstadt.
Konstan, D. 2001. "*To Hellênikon ethnos*: Ethnicity and the Construction of Ancient Greek Identity." In *Ancient Perceptions of Ethnicity*, edited by I. Malkin, 29–50. Cambridge, MA.
Kopanias, K. 2015. "The Mushki/Phrygian Problem from the Near Eastern Point of View." In *Nostoi: Indigenous Culture, Migration, and Integration in the Aegean Islands and Western Anatolia during the Bronze and Early Iron Ages*, edited by N. Stampolidis, Ç. Maner, and K. Kopanias, 211–25. Istanbul.
Kopanias, K. 2021. *Ahhiyawa: Το Μυκηναϊκό Αιγαίο μέσα από τα Χεττιτικά Κείμενα.* Athens.
Kosmetatou, E. 1995. "The Legend of the Hero Pergamus." *AncSoc* 26: 133–44.
Kosmetatou, E. 1997a. "Pisidia and the Hellenistic Kings." *AncSoc* 28: 5–37.
Kosmetatou, E. 1997b. "The Hero Solymos on the Coinage of Termessos Major." *SNR* 76: 41–62.
Kosmetatou, E. 2001. "Ilion, the Troad, and the Attalids." *AncSoc* 31: 107–32.
Kosmetatou, E. 2003. "The Attalids of Pergamon." In *A Companion to the Hellenistic World*, edited by A. Erskine, 159–74. Oxford.
Kosmetatou, E. 2005. "Macedonians in Pisidia." *Historia* 54.2: 216–21.
Kosmetatou, E. and M. Waelkens. 1997. "The 'Macedonian' Shields of Sagalassos." In *Sagalassos IV (1994 and 1995)*, edited by M. Waelkens and J. Poblone. Leuven.
Kosmin, P. 2019. "Remaking a City: Sardis in the Long Third Century." In *Spear-Won Land: Sardis from the King's Peace to the Peace of Apamea*, edited by A. Berlin and P. Kosmin, 75–90. Madison.
Kuttner, A. 2005. "Do You Look like You Belong Here? Asianism at Pergamon and the Makedonian Diaspora." In *Cultural Borrowings and Ethnic Appropriation in Antiquity*, edited by E. Gruen, 137–206. Stuttgart.
Labarre, G. 2009. "Les origines et la diffusion du culte de Men." In *L'Asie Mineure dans l'antiquité: Échanges, populations et territoires*, edited by H. Bru, F. Kirbihler, and S. Lebreton, 389–414. Rennes.
Labarre, G. et al. 2015. "Colonisation et interculturalité en Pisidie et Phrygie Parorée." *Epigraphica Anatolica* 48: 87–114.
LaBuff, J. 2013. "Who(')s(e) Karian? Language, Names, and Identity." *AHB* 27.3-4: 86–107.
LaBuff, J. 2016. *Polis Expansion and Elite Power in Hellenistic Karia.* Lanham, MD.
LaBuff, J. 2017. "The Achaemenid Creation of Karia." In *The History of the Argeads: New Perspectives*, edited by S. Müller, T. Howe, H. Bowden, and R. Rollinger, 27–40. Wiesbaden.
LaBuff, J. Forthcoming. "Leagues of Carians as Local rather than Imperial Structures." In *Hellenistic Monarchies*, edited by M. Munn, S. Redford, and D. Redford. Berlin.
La'da, C. 2002. *Foreign Ethnics in Hellenistic Egypt.* Leuven.

Laminger-Pascher, G. 1989. *Lykaonien und die Phryger*. Vienna.
Laroche, D. 2007. "La reconstruction du temple de Létô au Létôon de Xanthos." *RA*: 169–74.
Laroche, E. 1976. "Lyciens et Termiles." *RA*: 15–19.
Laumonier, A. 1958. *Les cultes indigènes de Carie*. Paris.
Launey, M. 1949. *Recherche sur les armées hellénistiques*. Paris.
Leonhard, R. 1915. *Paphlagonia: Reisen und Forschungen im nördlichen Kleinasien*. Berlin.
Le Roy, C. 1989. "Aspects du plurilinguisme dans la Lycie antique." *Anadolu* 22: 217–26.
Le Roy, C. 1991. "Le développement du Létôon de Xanthos." *RA*: 341–51.
Le Roy, C. 1996. "Une convention entre cités en lycie du nord." *CRAI* 3: 961–80.
Le Roy, C. 2004. "Dieux anatoliens et dieux grecs en Lycie." In *Les cultes locaux dans les mondes grec et romain*, edited by G. Labarre, 263–74. Lyon.
Le Roy, C. 2005. "Vocabulaire grec et institutions Locales Dans l'Asie Mineure Achéménide." In *Democrazia e Antidemocrazia nel mondo greco*, edited by U. Bultrighini, 333–44. Alexandria.
Llewelyn-Jones, L. and J. Robson. 2010. *Ctesias' History of Persia: Tales of the Orient*. New York.
Lloyd-Jones, H. 1999. "The Pride of Halicarnassus." *ZPE* 124: 1–14.
López-Ruiz, C. 2009. "Mopsos and Cultural Exchange between Greeks and Locals in Cilicia." In *Antiken Mythen: Medien, Transformationen und Konstruktionen*, edited by U. Dill and C. Walde, 487–501. Berlin.
Lozano Velilla, A. 2006. "Nacionalismo versus ciudadanía. El caso de Caria." In *La construcción ideológica de la ciudadanía*, edited by D. Plácido Suárez, 359–80. Madrid.
Lulli, L. 2016. "The Fight of Telephus: Poetic Visions behind the Pergamon Frieze." In *The Look of Lyric: Greek Song and the Visual*, edited by V. Cazzato and A. Lardinois, 50–68. Leiden.
Ma, J. 2003. "Peer Polity Interaction in the Hellenistic World." *P&P* 180: 9–39.
Ma, J. 2008. "Mysians on the Çan Sarcophagos? Ethnicity and Domination in Achaemenid Military Art." *Historia* 57.3: 243–54.
Mac Sweeney, N. 2011. *Community Identity and Archaeology: Dynamic Communities at Aphrodisias and Beycesultan*. Ann Arbor.
Mac Sweeney, N. 2013. *Foundation Myths and Politics in Ancient Ionia*. Cambridge.
Mac Sweeney, N. 2015. "Violence and the Ionian Migration: Representation and Reality." In *Nostoi: Indigenous Culture, Migration, and Integration in the Aegean Islands and Western Anatolia during the Bronze and Early Iron Ages*, edited by N. Stampolidis, Ç. Maner, and K. Kopanias, 239–59. Istanbul.
Mac Sweeney, N. 2017. "Separating Fact from Fiction in the Ionian Migration." *Hesperia* 86: 379–421.

Mac Sweeney, N. 2021. "Regional Identities in the Greek World: Myth and Koinon in Ionia." *Historia* 70.3: 268–314.

Maddoli, G. 2010. "Du nouveau sur les Hékatomnides d'après les inscriptions de Iasos." In *Hellenistic Karia*, edited by R. van Bremen and J.-M. Carbon, 123–31. Pessac.

Malay, H. 1990. "Some Mysians from Emoddi." *EA* 16: 65–67.

Malay, H. 1999. *Researches in Lydia, Mysia, and Aiolis*. Vienna.

Marchese, R. 1989. *The Historical Archaeology of Northern Caria*. Oxford.

Marek, C. 2003. Pontus et Bithynia: *Die römischen Provinzen im Norden Kleinasiens*. Mainz.

Marek, C. 2009. "Hellenisation and Romanisation in Pontos-Bithynia: An Overview." In *Mithridates VI and the Pontic Kingdom*, edited by J. Højte, 35–46. Aarhus.

Marek, C. 2013. "Political Institutions and the Lykian and Karian Languages in the Process of Hellenization between the Achaemenids and the Diadochi." In *Shifting Social Imaginaries in the Hellenistic Period*, edited by E. Stavrianopoulou, 233–51. Leiden.

Marek, C. 2015. "Zum Charakter der Hekatomnidenherrschaft im Kleinasien des 4. Jh. v.Chr." In *Zwischen Satrapen und Dynasten: Kleinasien in 4. Jahrhundert v.Chr.*, edited by E. Winter and K. Zimmermann, 1–20. Bonn.

Marek, C., and P. Frei. 2016. *In the Land of a Thousand Gods: A History of Asia Minor in the Ancient World*. Translated by S. Rendall. Princeton.

Marqués, F. 2019. "A Clay Kybele in the City Center." In *Spear-Won Land: Sardis from the King's Peace to the Peace of Apamea*, edited by A. Berli and P. Kosmin, 120–31. Madison.

Massa, M. et al. 2020. "A Landscape-oriented Approach to Urbanisation and Early State Formation on the Konya and Karaman plains, Turkey." *AS* 70: 45–75.

McGing, B. 2014. "Iranian Kings in Greek Dress? Cultural Identity in the Mithridatid Kingdom of Pontos." In *Space, Place, and Identity in Northern Anatolia*, edited by T. Bekker-Nielsen, 21–37. Stuttgart.

McInerney, J. 2021. "Salmakis and the Priests of Halikarnassos." *Klio* 103.1: 59–89.

Mehl, A. 2003. "Xanto il lidio, i suoi Lydiaká e la Lidia." In *Licia e Lidia prima dell'ellenizzazione*, edited by M. Giorgieri, 245–52. Rome.

Melchert, T.C. 2003. *The Luwians*. Leiden.

Melchert, T.C. 2010. "Lydian Language and Inscriptions." In *The Lydians and Their World*, edited by N. Cahill, 267–72. Istanbul.

Mellink, M. 1970. "Archaeology in Asia Minor." *AJA* 74 (2): 157–78.

Meyer, M. 2001. "Cilicia as Part of the Seleukid Empire: The Beginning of Municipal Coinage." In *La Cilicie: Éspaces et pouvoirs locaux*, edited by E. Jean, A. Dinol, and S. Durugönül, 505–18. Paris.

Meyer, M. 2004. "Das Ebene Kilikien bis zum Beginn der hellenistischen Zeit." In *Kulturbegegnung in einem Brückenland. Gottheiten und Kulte als Indikatoren von*

Akkulturationsprozessen in Ebenen Kilikien, edited by M. Meyer and R. Zeigler, 7–17. Bonn.

Michels, C. 2009. *Kulturtransfer und monarchischer "Philhellenismus": Bithynien, Pontos, und Kappadokien in hellenistischer Zeit*. Göttingen.

Michels, C. 2013. "The Spread of Polis Institutions in Hellenistic Cappadocia and the Peer Polity Interaction Model." In *Shifting Social Imaginaries in the Hellenistic Period*, edited by E. Stavrianopoulou, 283–307. Leiden.

Michels, C. 2017. "The Persian Impact on Bithynia, Commagene, Pontus, and Cappadocia." In *The History of the Argeads: New Perspectives*, edited by S. Müller et al., 41–55. Wiesbaden.

Michels, C. 2020. "*Pepaideumenoi* and *Paideia* at the Court of Hellenistic Cappadocia and the Impact of Cultural Change." In *Greek* Paideia *and Local Tradition in the Graeco-Roman East*, edited by M.P. de Hoz, J. García Alonso, and L. Guichard Romero, 19–38. Leuven.

Mitchell, S. 1991. "The Hellenization of Pisidia." *MedArch* 4: 119–45.

Mitchell, S. 1992. "Hellenismus in Pisidien." In *Forschungen in Pisidien*, edited by E. Schwertheim, 1–27. Bonn.

Mitchell, S. 1993. *Anatolia: Land, Men, and Gods in Asia Minor*. Vol. 1. *The Celts in Anatolia and the Impact of Roman Rule*. Oxford.

Mitchell, S. 2000. "Ethnicity, Acculturation, and Empire in Roman and Late Roman Asia Minor." In *Ethnicity and Culture in Late Antiquity*, edited by S. Mitchell and G. Greatrex, 117–50. Swansea.

Mitchell, S. 2002. "In Search of the Pontic Community in Antiquity." In *Representations of Empire: Rome and the Mediterranean World*, edited by A. Bowman et al., 35–64. Oxford.

Mitchell, S. 2007. "Iranian Names and the Presence of Persians in the Religious Sanctuaries of Asia Minor." In *Old and New Worlds in Greek Onomastics*, edited by E. Matthews, 151–71. Oxford.

Mitchell, S. 2010. "The Ionians of Paphlagonia." In *Local Knowledge and Microidentities in the Imperial Greek World*, edited by T. Whitmarsh, 86–110. Cambridge.

Mitchell, S. 2017. "The Greek Impact in Asia Minor." In *Hellenism and the Local Communities of the Eastern Mediterranean. 400 BCE–250 CE*, edited by B. Chrubasik and D. King, 13–28. Oxford.

Mørkholm, O., and J. Zahle. 1972. "The Coinage of KuprLLi: Numismatic and Archaeological Studies." *AArch* 43: 57–113.

Mørkholm, O., and J. Zahle 1976. "The Coinages of the Lycian Dynasts Kheriga, Kherêi, and Erbbina." *AArch* 47: 47–90.

Muscarella, O. 2013. "The Iron Age Background to the Formation of the Phrygian State." In *Archaeology, Artifacts, and Antiquities of the Ancient Near East: Sites, Cultures, Proveniences*, edited by O. Muscarella, 549–68. Leiden.

Mutafian, C. 1988. *La Cilicie au carrefour des empires*. Paris.
Nafissi, M. 2015. "Königliche Ansprüche der Hekatomniden: Das neue Monument für die Basileis Kariens aus Iasos." In *Zwischen Satrapen und Dynasten: Kleinasien in 4. Jahrhundert v.Chr.*, edited by E. Winter and K. Zimmermann, 21–98. Bonn.
Naour, C. 1981. "Inscriptions du moyen Hermos." *ZPE* 44: 11–41.
Nijf, O. van. 2010. "Being Termessian: Local Knowledge and Identity Politics in a Pisidian City." In *Local Knowledge and Microidentities in the Imperial Greek World*, edited by T. Whitmarsh, 163–88. Oxford.
Nilsson, M. 1906. *Griechische Feste*. Leipzig.
Nollé, J. 1983. "Die 'Charaktere' in 3, Epidemien Buch des Hippokrates und Mnemon von Side." *EA* 2: 85–98.
Novakova, L. 2017. "Tombs, Images, and Identities in Ancient Anatolia." *ILIRIA International Review* 7.2: 261–72.
Novakova, L. 2019. *Greeks Who Dwelt beyond the Sea: People, Places, Monuments*. Bonn.
Oettinger, N. 2008. "The Seer Mopsos (Muksas) as a Historical Figure." In *Anatolian Interfaces: Hittites, Greeks and Their Neighbours*, edited by B.J. Collins, M. Bachvarova, and I. Rutherford, 63–66. Oxford.
Olshausen, E. 1974. "Zum Hellenisierungsprozess am pontischen Königshof." *AncSoc* 5: 153–70.
Oreshko, R. 2013. "Hipponax and the Linguistic, Ethnic, and Religious Milieu of Western Anatolia." *Hephaistos* 30: 79–104.
Oreshko, R. 2017. "Hartapu and the Land of Masa." *Altorientalische Forschungen* 44: 47–67.
Oreshko, R. 2018. "Ahhiyawa and Danu(Na): Greek Ethnic Groups in the Eastern Mediterranean in Light of Old and New Hieroglyphic-Luwian Evidence." In *Change, Continuity, and Connectivity: North-Eastern Mediterranean at the Turn of the Bronze Age and in the Early Iron Age*, edited by L. Niesiolowski-Spano and M. Wecowski, 23–56. Wiesbaden.
Oreshko, R. 2019. "Geography of the Western Fringes: Gar(a)Gisa/Gargiya and the Lands of the Late Bronze Age Karia." In *KARIA ARKHAIA: La Carie, des origines à la période pré-hékatomnide*, edited by O. Henry and K. Konuk, 139–90. Istanbul.
Oreshko, R. 2020. "Ethnic Groups and Ethnic Contacts in Lycia (I): The Maritime Interface." *Journal of Language Relationship* 18: 13–40.
Panichi, S. 2005. "Cappadocia through Strabo's Eyes." In *Strabo's Cultural Geography*, edited by D. Dueck, H. Lindsay, and S. Pothecary, 200–215. Cambridge.
Paradiso, A. 2007. "Sur la servitude volontaire des Mariandyniens d'Héraclée du Pont." In *Fear of Slaves, Fear of Enslavement in the Ancient Mediterranean = Peur de l'esclave, peur de l'esclavage en Méditerranée ancienne (discours, représentations, pratiques)*, edited by A. Serghidou, 23–33. Besançon.

Parker, R. 2000. "Theophoric Names and the History of Greek Religion." In *Greek Personal Names: Their Value as Evidence*, edited by S. Hornblower and E. Matthews, 53–80. Oxford.

Parker, R. 2018. "Caria and Polis Religion." In *Πλειών. Papers in Memory of Christiane Sourvinou-Inwood*, edited by A. Kavoulaki, 33–57. Rethymno.

Pavúk, P. 2015. "Between Aegeans and Hittites: Western Anatolia in the Second Millennium BC." In *Nostoi: Indigenous Culture, Migration, and Integration in the Aegean Islands and Western Anatolia during the Bronze and Early Iron Ages*, edited by N. Stampolidis, Ç. Maner, and K. Kopanias, 81–113. Istanbul.

Payne, A. 2006. "Multilingual Inscriptions and Their Audiences: Cilicia and Lycia." In *Margins of Writing, Origins of Cultures*, edited by S. Sanders, 121–36. Chicago.

Payne, A. 2012. *Iron Age Hieroglyphic Inscriptions*. Atlanta.

Payne, A. 2019. "Native Religious Traditions from a Lydian Perspective." In *Religious Convergence in the Ancient Mediterranean*, edited by B. Collins and S. Blakely, 231–48. Atlanta.

Payne, A., and J. Wintjes. 2016. *Lords of Asia Minor: An Introduction to the Lydians*. Wiesbaden.

Pedersen, P. 2013. "The 4th Century BC 'Ionian Renaissance' and Karian Identity." In *4th-Century Karia: Defining a Karian Identity under the Hekatomnids*, edited by O. Henry, 33–64. Istanbul.

Petrova, A. 1998. "Bryges and Phrygians." In *Thracians and Phrygians: Problems of Parallelism*, edited by N. Tuna, Z. Aktüre, and M. Lynch, 45–54. Ankara.

Petzl, G. 2019. "Zum Inschriftencorpus von Sardeis – einem Vorhaben Peter Herrmanns." In *Epigraphische Notizen: Zur Erinnerung an Peter Herrmann*, edited by K. Harter-Uibopuu, 13–27. Stuttgart.

Piras, D. 2009. "Der archäologische Kontext karischer Sprachdenkmäler und seine Bedeutung für die kulturelle Identität Kariens." In *Die Karer und die Anderen*, edited by F. Rumscheid, 229–50. Bonn.

Piras, D. 2010. "Who Were the Karians in Hellenistic Times?" In *Hellenistic Karia*, edited by R. van Bremen and J.-M. Carbon, 217–33. Pessac.

Pohl, D. 2004a. "Baal und Zeus in Tarsos." In *Kulturbegegnung in einem Brückenland: Gottheiten und Kulte als Indikatoren von Akkulturationsprozessen in Ebenen Kilikien*, edited by M. Meyer and R. Ziegler, 63–73. Bonn.

Pohl, D. 2004b. "Sandan in Tarsos." In *Kulturbegegnung in einem Brückenland: Gottheiten und Kulte als Indikatoren von Akkulturationsprozessen in Ebenen Kilikien*, edited by M. Meyer and R. Ziegler, 73–93. Bonn.

Potter, D. 2007. "The Identities of Lykia." In *Regionalism in Hellenistic and Roman Asia Minor*, edited by H. Elton and G. Reger, 81–88. Bordeaux.

Prinz, F. 1979. *Gründungsmythen und Sagenchronologie*. Munich.

Prost, F. 2007. "Identité des peuples, identité des cités: L'exemple lycien." *Pallas* 73: 99–113.

Prost, F. 2013. "Retour au Mausolée et au monument des Neréides. Identités ethniques et frontières culturelles en Lycie et en Carie." In *Euploia. La Lycie et la Carie antiques. Dynamiques des territoires, échanges et identités*, edited by P. Brun et al., 175–86. Bordeaux.

Raimond, E. 2002. "Patara: Un foyer religieux aux Ier et IIe millénaires a.C." In *Panthéons ruraux de l'Asie Mineure pré-chrétienne*, edited by R. Lebrun, 195–215. Leuven.

Raimond, E. 2007. "Hellenization and Lycian Cults during the Achaemenid Period." In *Persian Responses: Political and Cultural Interaction with(in) the Achaemenid Empire*, edited by C. Tuplin, 143–62. Swansea.

Raimond, E. 2009. "Mythes, cultes et territoires en Lycie." In *L'Asie Mineure dans l'antiquité: Échanges, populations et territoires*, edited by H. Bru, F. Kirbihler, and S. Lebreton, 229–40. Rennes.

Ratté, C. 2009. "The Carians and the Lydians." In *Die Karer und Die Anderen*, edited by F. Rumscheid, 149–62. Bonn.

Reger, G. 2007. "Karia: A Case Study." In *Regionalism in Hellenistic and Roman Asia Minor*, edited by H. Elton and G. Reger, 89–96. Bordeaux.

Reger, G. 2011. "Interregional Economies in the Aegean Basin." In *The Economies of Hellenistic Societies: Third to First Centuries BC*, edited by Z. Archibald, J. Davies, and V. Gabrielsen, 368–90. Oxford.

Renberg, G. 2014. "Unexplored Aspects of the Lycian 'Twelve God Reliefs'." *EA* 47: 107–32.

Rens, R. 2015. "Public Squares for Barbarians? The Development of the *agorai* in Pisidia." In *Continuity and Destruction in the Greek East: The Transformation of Monumental Space from the Hellenistic Period to Late Antiquity*, edited by S. Chandrasekaran and A. Kouremenos, 11–32. Oxford.

Reynolds, J., and K. Erim. 1982. *Aphrodisias and Rome: Documents from the Excavation of the Theatre at Aphrodisias Conducted by Professor Kenan T. Erim, Together with Some Related Texts*. London.

Rivas, J. 2005. "Phrygian Tales." *GRBS* 45.3: 223–44.

Robert, L. 1937. *Études anatoliennes*. Paris.

Robert, L. 1962. *Villes d'Asie Mineure*. Paris.

Robert, L. 1963. *Noms indigènes dans l'Asie Mineure gréco-romaine*. Paris.

Robert, L. 1969. "Les inscriptions." In *Laodicée du Lycos. Le nymphée. Campagnes 1961–1963*, edited by J. Gagniers et al., 247–389. Paris.

Robert, L. 1976. "Monnaies grecques de l'époque impériale." *RN* 18: 25–56.

Robert, L. 1982. "Documents d'Asie Mineure." *BCH* 106: 395–543.

Robert, L. and J. Robert. 1954. *La Carie: Histoire et géographie historique avec le recueil des inscriptions antique*. Paris.

Rojas, F. 2013. "Antiquarianism in Roman Sardis." In *World Antiquarianism: Comparative Perspectives*, edited by A. Schnapp, 176–200. Los Angeles.

Rojas, F. 2019. *The Pasts of Roman Anatolia: Interpreters, Traces, Horizons*. Cambridge.

Roller, L. 1991. "The Great Mother at Gordion: The Hellenization of an Anatolian Cult." *JHS* 111: 128–43.

Roller, L. 1999. *In Search of God the Mother: The Cult of Anatolian Cybele*. Berkeley.

Roller, L. 2011. "Phrygia and Phrygians." In *The Oxford Handbook of Ancient Anatolia*, edited by S. Steadman and G. McMahon, 560–78. Oxford.

Roller, L. 2012. "Phrygian Religion and Cult Practice." In *Phrygians: In the Land of Midas, in the Shadow of Monuments*, edited by T. Sivas and H. Sivas, 202–31. Istanbul.

Roller, L. 2014. "Attitudes Towards the Past in Roman Phrygia: Survivals and Revivals." In *Attitudes toward the Past: Creating Identities*, edited by B. Alroth and C. Scheffer, 241–42. Stockholm.

Rollinger, R. 2006. "Assyrios, Syrios, Syros, and Leukosyros." *WO* 36: 72–82.

Romeo, I. 2002. "The Panhellenion and Ethnic Identity in Hadrianic Greece." *CPh* 97.1: 21–40.

Roosevelt, C. 2003. "Lydian and Persian Period Settlement in Lydia." Ithaca.

Roosevelt, C. 2009. *The Archaeology of Lydia from Gyges to Alexander*. Cambridge.

Roosevelt, C. 2010. "Lydia before the Lydians." In *The Lydians and Their World*, edited by N. Cahill, 37–73. Istanbul.

Roosevelt, C. 2019. "The Inhabited Landscapes of Lydia." In *Spear-Won Land: Sardis from the King's Peace to the Peace of Apamea*, edited by A. Berlin and P. Kosmin, 145–64. Madison.

Rose. C.B. 2008. "Separating Fact from Fiction in the Aiolian Migration." *Hesperia* 77.3: 399–430.

Rousset, D. 2010. *Fouilles de Xanthos. 10. De Lycie en Cabalide: Le convention entre les Lyciens et Termessos près d'Oinoanda*. Geneva.

Ruby, P. 2006. "Peuples, fictions? Ethnicité, identités ethniques et societés anciennes." *REA* 108.1: 25–60.

Rumscheid, F. 2019. "Überlegungen zur materiellen Kultur Mylasas in archäischer Zeit." In *KARIA ARKHAIA: La Carie, des origines à la période pré-hékatomnide*, edited by O. Henry and K. Konuk, 309–26. Istanbul.

Rung, E. 2015. "The End of the Lydian Kingdom and the Lydians after Croesus." In *Political Memory in and after the Persian Empire*, edited by J. Silverman and C. Waerzeggers, 7–26. Atlanta.

Rutherford, I. 2002. "Interference or Translationese? Some Patterns in Lycian-Greek Bilingualism." In *Bilingualism in Ancient Society: Language Contact and the Written Text*, edited by J.N. Adams, M. Janse, and S. Swain, 197–219. Oxford.

Ruzicka, S. 1992. *Politics of a Persian Dynasty: The Hecatomnids in the Fourth Century B.C.* Norman, OK.

Şahın, N. 2016. "Gods and Cults of Lycia." In *Lukka'dan Likya'ya: Sarpedon ve Aziz Nikolaos'un Ülkesi/From Lukka to Lycia: The Land of Sarpedon and Saint Nicholaos*, edited by H. İşkan and E. Dündar, 536–49. Istanbul.

Salmeri, G. 2000. "Regioni, popoli, e lingue epicorie d'Asia Minore nella Geografica di Strabone." In *Strabone e l'Asia Minore*, edited by A. Biraschi and G. Salmeri, 157–88. Naples.

Salmeri, G. 2004. "Hellenism on the Periphery: The Case of Cilicia and an Etymology of Soloikismos." In *The Greco-Roman East: Politics, Culture, Society*, edited by S. Colvin, 181–206. Cambridge.

Salmeri, G. 2011. "Linguistic and Cultural Dynamics in Cilicia: A Summary." In *Hellenismus in der Kilikia Pedias*, edited by A. Hoffmann, R. Posamentir, and M. Sayar, 191–98. Istanbul.

Santini, M. 2016. "A Multi-Ethnic City Shapes Its Past. The 'Pride of Halicarnassos' and the Memory of Salmakis." *ASNP* 8.1: 3–35.

Santini, M. 2017. "Bellerophontes, Pegasos, and the Foundation of Halicarnassos. Contributions to the Study of the Salmakis Inscription." *SCO* 63: 109–43.

Sartre, M. 2003. *L'Anatolie hellénistique de l'Égée au Caucase (334–31 av. J.C.)*. Paris.

Sartre, M. 2007. "Romanisation en Asie Mineure?" In *Tra Oriente e Occidente. Indigeni, greci, e romani in Asia Minore*, edited by G. Urso, 229–45. Pisa.

Sauzeau, P. 1997. "Χρυσάωρ, χρυσάορος, et l'épée d'or de Déméter." *RPh* 71.1: 103–18.

Savalli-Lestrade, I. 2001. "I greci e i popoli dell'Anatolia." In *I Greci: Storia, cultura, arte, società*. Vol. 3. *I greci oltre la Grecia*, edited by S. Settis, 39–78. Turin.

Savalli-Lestrade, I. 2010. "Intitulés royaux et intitulés civiques." *Studi ellinistici* 24: 127–48.

Saviano, M. 2017. "Sui 'cari barbarofoni' di *Il*. II.867." *Erga-Logoi* 5 (2): 81–94.

Saviano, M. 2018. "Il santuario di Zeus Cario a Milasa: Alcune asservazioni." In *Studi di storia e storiografia greca offerti a Clara Talamo*, edited by M. Polito, 79–98. Canterano.

Sayar, M. 2004. "Das Ebene Kilikien vom Tod Alexanders des Großen bis zur Gründung der Provinz Cilicia durch Kaiser Vespasian." In *Kulturbegegnung in einem Brückenland. Gottheiten und Kulte als Indikatoren von Akkulturationsprozessen in Ebenen Kilikien*, edited by M. Meyer and R. Ziegler, 17–28. Bonn.

Sayar, M. 2007. "Historical Development of Urbanization in Cilicia in Hellenistic and Roman Periods." In *Tra Oriente e Occidente. Indigeni, greci e romani in Asia Minore*, edited by G. Urso, 247–57. Pisa.

Scheer, T. 1993. *Mythische Vorväter zur Bedeutung griechischer Heroenmythen im Selbstverständnis kleinasiatischer Städte*. Munich.

Schmitt, R. 2003. "Lyder und Lyker in den achaimenischen Quellen." In *Licia e Lidia prima dell'ellenizzazione*, edited by M.-C. Trémouille and P. Vannicelli, 290–300. Rome.

Scholten, J. 2007. "Building Hellenistic Bithynia." In *Regionalism in Hellenistic and Roman Asia Minor*, edited by H. Elton and G. Reger, 17–24. Bordeaux.

Schörner, H. 2005. "Grabarchitektur, Ausstattung und Beigaben als Indikatoren der Romanisierung/Romanisation in der römischen Provinz Asia am Beispiel des Grabbaues am Theater in Priene." In *Romanisierung – Romanisation: Theoretische Modelle und Praktische Fallbeispiele*, edited by G. Schörner, 219–34. Oxford.

Schuler, C. 1998. *Ländliche Siedlungen und Gemeinden im hellenistischen und römischen Kleinasien*. Munich.

Schuler, C. 2016. "Lycia and the Lycian League in the Hellenistic Period (Fourth–First Centuries BC)." In *Lukka'dan Likya'ya: Sarpedon ve Aziz Nikolaos'un Ülkesi/From Lukka to Lycia: The Land of Sarpedon and Saint Nicholaos*, edited by H. İşkan and E. Dündar, 46–59. Istanbul.

Schuler, C. 2019. "Lycian, Persian, Greek, Roman: Chronological Layers and Structural Developments in the Onomastics of Lycia." In *Changing Names: Tradition and Innovation in Ancient Greek Onomastics*, edited by R. Parker, 195–216. Oxford.

Schürr, D. 2007. "Formen der Akkulturation in Lykien: Griechische-lykische Sprachbeziehungen." In *Griechische Epigraphik in Lykien: Eine Zwischenbilanz*, edited by C. Schuler, 27–40. Vienna.

Schürr, D. 2013. "Über den Gebrauch der Schrift in Lykien." In *Euploia. La Lycie et la Carie antiques. Dynamiques des territoires, échanges et identités*, edited by P. Brun et al., 29–40. Bordeaux.

Schürr, D. 2016. "Neighbors of the Lycians: Solymoi, Rhodians, Milyai, Kabaleis, and Carians." In *Lukka'dan Likya'ya: Sarpedon ve Aziz Nikolaos'un Ülkesi/From Lukka to Lycia: The Land of Sarpedon and Saint Nicholaos*, edited by H. İşkan and E. Dündar, 100–09. Istanbul.

Schweyer, A. 1996. "Le pays lycien. Un étude de géographie historique aux époques classique et hellénistique." *Revue archéologique* 1: 3–68.

Seaman, K. 2020. *Rhetoric and Innovation in Hellenistic Art*. Cambridge.

Sears, M. 2014. "Alexander and Ada Reconsidered." *CPh* 109: 211–21.

Seel, G. 1956. "Lydiaka." *WS* 69: 212–36.

Sekunda, N. 1985. "Achaemenid Colonization in Lydia." *REA* 87: 7–30.

Sekunda, N. 1988. "Persian Settlement in Hellespontine Phrygia." In *Achaemenid History, III. Method and Theory*, edited by A. Kuhrt and H. Sancisi-Weerdenburg, 175–96. Leiden.

Sekunda, N. 1991. "Achaemenid Settlement in Caria, Lycia, and Greater Phrygia." In *Achaemenid History, VI. Asia Minor and Egypt. Old Cultures in a New Empire*, edited by H. Sancisi-Weerdenburg and A. Kuhrt, 83–143. Leiden.

Siapkas, J. 2014. "Ancient Ethnicity and Modern Identity." In *A Companion to Ethnicity in the Ancient Mediterranean*, edited by J. McInerney, 66–81. West Sussex.

Simon, Z. 2011. "Against the Identification of Karkisa with Carians." In *Nostoi: Indigenous Culture, Migration, and Integration in the Aegean Islands and Western Anatolia during the Bronze and Early Iron Ages*, edited by N. Stampolides, Ç. Maner, and K. Kopanias, 791–809. Istanbul.

Simon, Z. 2012. "Where Is the Land of Sura of the Hieroglyphic Luwian Inscription KARKAMIŠ A4b and Why Were Cappadocians Called Syrians by Greeks?" *Alteorientalische Forschungen* 39: 167–80.

Simon, Z. 2017. "Selected Pisidian Problems and the Position of Pisidian within the Anatolian Languages." *Journal of Language Relationship* 15.1–2: 31–42.

Singer, I. 1983. "Western Anatolia in the Thirteenth Century B.C. according to the Hittite Sources." *Anatolian Studies* 33: 205–17.

Skinner, J. 2012. *The Invention of Greek Ethnography: From Homer to Herodotus*. Oxford.

Smith, A. 1986. *The Ethnic Origins of Nations*. Oxford.

Sourvinou-Inwood, C. 2005. *Hylas, the Nymphs, Dionysos, and Others: Myth, Ritual, Ethnicity*. Stockholm.

Spawforth, A. 2001. "Shades of Greekness: A Lydian Case Study." In *Ancient Perceptions of Greek Ethnicity*, edited by I. Malkin, 375–400. Cambridge, MA.

Stewart, A. 1996. "Telephos/Telepinu and Dionysos: A Distant Light on an Ancient Myth." In *Pergamon: The Telephos Frieze from the Great Altar*, edited by R. Dreyfus and E. Schraudolph, 2: 109–19. San Francisco.

Strobel, K. 1996. *Die Galater: Geschichte und Eigenart der keltischen Staatenbildung auf dem Boden des hellenistischen Kleinasien. Band 1. Untersuchungen zur Geschichte und historischen Geographie des hellenistischen und römischen Kleinasien I*. Berlin.

Strobel, K. 2001. "Phryger-Lyder-Meder-Perser: Politische, ethnische, und kultural Größen Zentralanatoliens bei Errichtung der achaimenidischen Herrschaft." In *Achaemenid Anatolia*, edited by T. Bakir et al., 43–55. Leiden.

Strobel, K. 2002. "State Formation by the Galatians of Asia Minor. Politico-Historical and Cultural Processes in Hellenistic Central Anatolia." *Anatolica* 28: 1–46.

Strobel, K. 2009. "The Galatians in the Roman Empire: Historical Tradition and Ethnic Identity in Hellenistic and Roman Asia Minor." In *Ethnic Constructs in Antiquity: The Role of Power and Tradition*, edited by T. Derks and N. Roymans, 117–44. Amsterdam.

Stroud, R. 1984. "An Argive Decree from Nemea concerning Aspendos." *Hesperia* 53: 193–216.

Strubbe, J. 1984. "Gründer kleinasiatischer Städte: Fiktion und Realität." *AncSoc* 15/17: 253–309.

Strubbe, J. 1997. *ΑΡΑΙ ΕΠΙΤΥΜΒΙΟΙ: Imprecations against Desecrators of the Grave in the Greek Epitaphs of Asia Minor: A Catalogue*. Bonn.

Summerer, L. 2005. "Amisos – eine griechische Polis im Land der Leukosyrer." In *Pont-Euxin et Polis*, edited by D. Kacharova, M. Faudot, and E. Geny, 129–65. Franc-Comtoisés.

Summers, G.D. 2013. "East of the Halys: Thoughts on Settlement Patterns and Historical Geography in the Late Second Millennium and First Half of the First Millennium B.C." In *L'Anatolie des peuples, des cités et des cultures (IIe millenaire av. J.C.–Ve siècle ap. J.C.)*. Vol. 1. *Autour d'un projet d'atlas historique et archéologique de l'Asie Mineure. Méthodologie et prospective*, edited by H. Bru and G. Labarre: 41–51. Franché-Compté.

Summers, G.D. 2018. "Phrygians East of the Red River: Phrygianisation, Migration and Desertion." *AS* 68: 99–118.

Syme, R. 1995. *Anatolica: Studies in Strabo*. Edited by A. Birley. Oxford.

Talamo, C. 1979. *La Lidia arcaica*. Bologna.

Talloen, P. 2015. *Cult in Pisidia. Religious Practice in Southwest Asia Minor from Alexander the Great to the Rise of Christianity*. Turnhout.

Talloen, P., J. Pablone, M. Waelkens, and H. Vanhaverbeke. 2006. "Mater in Pisidia: Phrygian Influences in Southwestern Anatolia." In *Pluralismus und Wandel in den Religionen im vorhellenistichen Anatolien*, edited by M. Hutter and S. Hutter-Braunsar, 175–190. Münster.

Tanaka, K. 2018. "Anatolia in the Gap: Phrygia, Lydia, and Orientalizing Reconsidered." PhD. Dissertation. University of Pennsylvania.

Tavernier, J. 2015. "Des lyciens à Persepolis et en Mésopotamie durant la période achéménide (ca. 521–331 avant J.-C.)." *Hethica* 17: 147–74.

Tekoğlu, R. et al. 2000. "La bilingue royale louvito-phénicienne de Çineköy." *CRAI* 144 (3): 961–1007.

Tempesta, C. 2013. "Central and Local Powers in Hellenistic Rough Cilicia." In *Rough Cilicia: New Historical and Archaeological Approaches*, edited by M. Hoff and R. Townsend, 27–42. Oxford.

Thierry, N. 2002. *La Cappadoce de l'Antiquité au Moyen Âge*. Turnhout.

Thonemann, P. 2013. "Phrygia: An Anarchist History, 950 BC–100 AD." In *Roman Phrygia: Culture and Society*, edited by P. Thonemann, 1–40. Cambridge.

Thonemann, P. 2020. "A New 'Lydian History' from Sardis." *ZPE* 213: 78–84.

Tobin, J. 2001. "The Tarcondimotid Dynasty in Smooth Cilicia." In *La Cilicie: Éspaces et pouvoirs locaux*, edited by E. Jean, A. Dinçol, and S. Durugönül, 381–87. Paris.

Trampedach, K. 2011. "Die Neuordnung der Provinz Kilikien durch Pompeius (67–63 v.Chr.)." In *Hellenismus in der Kilikia Pedias*, edited by A. Hoffmann, R. Posamentir, and M. Sayar, 247–57. Istanbul.

Unwin, N.C. 2017. *Caria and Crete in Antiquity*. Cambridge.

Unwin, N.C. 2019. "Multilingualism in Karia and the Social Dynamics of Linguistic Assimilation." In *KARIA ARKHAIA: La Carie, des origines à la période préhékatomnide*, edited by O. Henry and K. Konuk, 43–60. Istanbul.

Vandorpe, K. 2000. "Negotiators' Laws from Rebellious Sagalassos in an Early Hellenistic Inscription." In *Sagalassos V*, edited by M. Waelken and L. Loots, 489–508. Leuven.

Vanhaverbeke, H., and M. Waelkens. 2005. "'If You Can't Beat Them, Join Them?' The Hellenization of Pisidia." *MedArch* 18: 49–65.

Vanhaverbeke, H. et al. 2010. "'Pisidian' Culture? The Classical-Hellenistic Site at Düzen Tepe near Sagalassus (Southwest Turkey)." *AS* 60: 105–28.

Vitale, M. 2014. "'Pontic' Communities under Roman Rule: Polis Self-Representation." In *Space, Place, and Identity in Northern Anatolia*, edited by T. Bekker-Nielsen, 49–61. Stuttgart.

Vitucci, G. 1953. *Il regno di Bithinia*. Rome.

Vlassopoulos, K. 2007. *Unthinking the Greek Polis: Ancient Greek History beyond Eurocentrism*. Cambridge.

Vlassopoulos, K. 2011. "Regional Perspectives and the Study of Greek History." *IncidAntico* 9: 9–31.

Vlassopoulos, K. 2015. "Ethnicity and Greek History: Re-examining our Assumptions." *BICS* 58: 1–13.

Voigt, M. 2011. "Gordion: The Changing Political and Economic Roles of a First Millennium City." In *The Oxford Handbook of Ancient Anatolia*, edited by S. Steadman and G. McMahon, 1069–1094. Oxford.

Voigt, M. and R. Henrickson. 2000. "Formation of the Phrygian State: The Early Iron Age at Gordion." *AS* 50: 37–54.

Voigtländer, W. "Vorläufer des Maussolleion." In *Architecture and Society in Hecatomnid Caria*, edited by T. Linders, 51–62. Uppsala.

Waelkens, M. 2013. "Euploia: Exchange and Identity in Ancient Caria and Lycia. Concluding Remarks." In *Euploia. La Lycie et la Carie antiques. Dynamiques des territoires, échanges et identités*, edited by P. Brun et al., 385–438. Bordeaux.

Webb, P. 1996. *Hellenistic Architectural Sculpture: Figural Motifs in Western Anatolia and the Aegean Islands*. Madison.

Weber, G. 1998–1999. "The Hellenistic Rulers and their Poets. Silencing Dangerous Critics?" *AncSoc* 29: 147–74.

Weiß, P. 1984. "Lebendiger Mythos. Gründerheroen und städtische Gründungstraditionen im griechisch-römischen Osten." *WJA* 10: 179–211.

Weiß, P. 1995. "Götter, Städte und Gelehrte: Lydiaka und 'Patria' um Sardes und den Tmolos." In *Forschungen in Lydien*, edited by E. Schwertheimer, 85–109. Bonn.

Welwei, K.-W. 2008. "Ursprung, Verbreitung, und Formen der Unfreiheit abhängiger Landbewohner im antiken Griechenland." In *Unfreie und abhängige Landbevölkerung*, edited by E. Herrmann-Otto, 1–52. Zurich.

White, R. 1991. *The Middle Ground: Indians, Empires, and Republics in the Great Lakes Region, 1650–1815*. Cambridge.

Widmer, P. 2004. "Λυδία: Ein Toponym zwischen Orient und Okzident." *HSF* 117.2: 197–203.

Williamson, C. 2016. "A Carian Shrine in a Hellenising World: The Sanctuary of Sinuri." In *Between Tarhuntas and Zeus Polieus: Cultural Crossroads in the Temples and Cults of Graeco-Roman Anatolia*, edited by M.P. de Hoz, J.P. Sanchez Hernández, and C. Molina Valero, 75–99. Leuven.

Williamson, C. 2021. *Urban Rituals in Sacred Landscapes in Hellenistic Asia Minor*. Leiden.

Wittke, A.-M. 2004. *Musker und Phryger: Ein Beitrag zur Geschichte Anatoliens vom 12. bis zum 7. Jh. v. Chr.* Wiesbaden.

Woolf, G. 1994. "Becoming Roman, Staying Greek: Culture, Identity, and the Civilizing Process in the Roman East." *Proceedings of the Cambridge Philological Society* 40: 116–43.

Woolf, G. 2010. "The Local and the Global in the Graeco-Roman East." In *Local Knowledge and Microidentities in the Imperial Greek World*, edited by T. Whitmarsh, 189–2000. Cambridge.

Wörrle, M. 1977. "Epigraphische Forschungen zur Geschichte Lykiens, I." *Chiron* 7: 43–66.

Wörrle, M. 1978. "Epigraphische Forschungen zur Geschichte Lykiens, II: Ptolemaios II. und Telmessos." *Chiron* 8: 201–46.

Wörrle, M. 1991. "Epigraphische Forschungen zur Geschichte Lykiens, 4: Drei Griechische Inschriften aus Limyra." *Chiron* 26: 202–39.

Woudhuizen, Fred. 1984–85. "Origins of the Sidetic Script." *Talanta* 16–17: 115–17.

Xydopoulos, I. 2007. "The Thracian Image in Herodotus and the Rhetoric of Otherness." In *Mediterranean Constructs*, edited by S. Antoniadou and A. Pace, 593–604. Athens.

Yağcı, R. 2013. "Problematizing Greek Colonization in the Eastern Mediterranean in the Seventh and Sixth Centuries BC: The Case of Soli." In *Rough Cilicia: New Historical and Archaeological Approaches*, edited by M. Hoff and R. Townsend, 6–15. Oxford.

Yakubovitch, I. 2008. "Luwian Migration in Light of Linguistic Contacts." In *Anatolian Interfaces: Hittites, Greeks and Their Neighbours*, edited by B.J. Collins, M. Bachvarova, and I. Rutherford, 123–34. Oxford.

Yakubovitch, I. 2010. *Sociolinguistics of the Luwian Language*. Leiden.

Yakubovitch, I. 2015. "Phoenician and Luwian in Iron Age Cilicia." *AS* 65: 35–53.

Yegül, F. 2019. "The Temple of Artemis." In *Spear-Won Land: Sardis from the King's Peace to the Peace of Apamea*, edited by A. Berlin and P. Kosmin, 132–42. Madison.

Younger, K. 1998. "The Phoenician Inscription of Azatiwada: An Integrated Reading." *Journal of Semitic Studies* 43: 11–47.

Zimmermann, M. 1992. *Untersuchungen zur historischen Landeskunde Zentrallykiens*. Bonn.

Ziskowski, A. 2014. "The Bellerophon Myth in Early Corinthian History and Art." *Hesperia* 83: 81–102.

Zurbach, J. 2019. "Miletos, a Great City and the Social Tensions of the Archaic Period." In *KARIA ARKHAIA: La Carie, des origines à la période pré-hékatomnide*, edited by O. Henry and K. Konuk, 247–56. Istanbul.

Index of Ancient Sources

Inscriptions

CIG 3456	73
FD III.4	
132, 134	70
163	26
Fontrier 1896, #2	42
Gusmani et al. 2002	
#40, #48, #52	14n28
IG I³	
266	33
268, 273	23
IG XII.4.1 209	38
IGR IV.1515	73
IMylasa 106	25
IStratonikeia 27	27n94
IvP 1	
1	16n32
245	23n73
İplikçioğlu, Çelgin, & Çelgin 2007	
#13, #17	47
Isager 1998 (Salmakis inscription)	
	29n101
KAI 26	51
Karkamish A6	48
Keil & Premerstein 1914	
#142	42
Labraunda 5	26
LW	
11	16
1, 2, 24, 25, 54	17
MAMA VIII.418b	27n91
Milet I	
2.3	74
3.43	61n260
OGIS	
234	75
565	37n148
Petzl 2019	
#577, #578	20n61
Persian Royal Inscriptions (*DSz, DSaa, DB, Dpe, DNa, Dse, XPh*)	
	10
SEG 9.484	59n253
*SIG*³	
167	25
279	42
Stroud 1984	66n281
TAM	
2.174, 555	32
2.247, 905	37n148
5.1.202, 240	59n253
5.1.444, 690	23
5.2.1233	20n
5.3.1540	59n253
Tekoğlu et al. 2000	51
TL 44	33–34

Greek and Latin Authors

Aischylos
Persians
  49–52   15n31

Alexander Polyhistor (*FGrH* 273)
  F58   32

THE PEOPLES OF ANATOLIA

Apollodoros
   3.1.2   50

Aristophanes
   Knights   49n215

Aristotle
   fr. 548   35

Arrian (*FGrH* 156)
   F77a   38–39

Bacchylides
   3   18n47

Cicero
In Verrem
   1.95   45

Dio Chrystostom
Orationes
   39.1   87

Diodoros
   11.60.4   33n127

Hell. Oxy.
   16.1   24

Hekataios of Miletos (*FGrH* 1)
   F1, F10   32

Herodotos
   1.7   12
   1.72   47
   1.94   15, 22
   1.125   15n31
   1.144   7
   1.146.2   29n101
   1.171   22, 24
   1.172   63
   1.173   31
   1.176   32
   2.2   41
   3.89–90   7, 37, 45, 47, 49–50
   3.93   7n8
   5.49.6   47, 50
   5.88, 119.2   25
   7.72   7, 47, 49
   7.73   7, 41
   7.74   7, 12, 21
   7.75   7, 37
   7.76   7
   7.77   7, 45, 50
   7.91   7, 47, 50, 65n280, 66
   7.92–95   7
   7.101–02   66
   7.110   37
   8.144   11

Homer
Iliad
   2.862–63   41n166
   2.864   12
   6.119–236   31
   13.3–5   21, 41
   13.793   41n166
   18.290–92   41n166
   24.544–46   41n166

Menekrates of Xanthos (*FGrH* 769)
   F1   32

Metrophanes (*FGrH* 796)
         44

Mimnermos
   13   18n47

Nikolaos of Damascus (*FGrH* 90)
   F15   15n30

Panyassis of Halikarnassos
   fr. 18 Kinkel   32

Pausanias
   5.1.26   49–50

Philip of Theangela (*FGrH* 741)
   F1   28

Pliny the elder
Naturalis Historia
   5.94   50

Polycharmos (*FGrH* 770)
   F5   32

Pseudo-Skylax
  94   42
  101–102   66

Sappho
  16, 96   18n47

Schol.ad Apoll.Rh.
  1.1115   60

Skylax
  F11   37

Strabo
  7.3.2   21
  12.1.1–2   48
  12.1.3   43n182
  12.1.5   40
  12.2.3   48
  12.2.6   48
  12.2.11   48–49
  12.3.3   21, 37, 60
  12.3.4, 12, 40   49
  12.3.9   43n182, 49
  12.4.1   21, 43n182
  12.4.4   21, 39, 43n182
  12.4.8   37
  12.6.1–5   47
  12.7.2   43n182
  12.8.3   21
  12.8.4   22
  12.8.9   24
  12.8.13   43n182, 44
  13.4.6   13
  13.4.12   13, 43n182
  13.4.9, 11   14n25
  13.4.12   27n92
  13.4.15–16   45
  13.4.17   13–14, 45
  14.1.38   27n92
  14.1.42   27n92, 61n260
  14.2.25   26, 86
  14.3.3   13
  14.4.3   47
  14.4.4–5   66
  14.5.1, 24   50
  14.5.22   43n182
  15.5.1–21   50

Tacitus
Annales
  4.55   20

Thucydides
  3.104   25n82

Xanthos (*FGrH* 765)
  F8   24n80
  F15   12, 15, 21
  F16   12
  F20   73

Xenophon
Anabasis
  1.1.11   45
  7.8.25   47

Cyropaideia
  6.2.10   47

General Index

acculturation model, critique of   67–69, 72–73
Aiolians. *See* Greeks
Alabanda   75, 88
Amyzon   60
  cult of Artemis   30, 80
Antiocheia by Pisidia   8, 87
Antiocheia on the Maeander   88
Apameia   8, 44
Aphrodisias   8, 27, 43n182, 75
Apollo
  Kataonian. *See* Kataonians
  in Lykia   36, 62
  Patroos in Patara   37
architectural style and Hellenization   82
  in Karia   25, 30
  in Lykia   36
  in Phrygia   41

Ariarathid dynasty 48, 78–79, 84
   royal foundations 88
Armenians 3, 7n8
Artemis
   in Lykia 36, 80
   of Amyzon. *See* Amyzon
   of Ephesos. *See* Ephesos
   of Sardis. *See* Sardis
Aspendos 66
Assyrian Empire 10n9
   textual evidence 41–42, 50, 65
Athens 21, 73
Attalid dynasty 21, 78
   colonization 19, 21
   Mysian military units 23–24
   Telephos myth, use of 22–23, 74
Attarimna 62

Balboura 8, 46
Bellerophon 26, 29n, 31–32, 63, 76
Bithynian kingdom 38–39, 90
   royal foundations 39, 88
burial evidence 53
   and Hellenization 82–83
   Çan sarcophagus 24
   Lydian tumuli 17, 20
   Karian chamber tombs 30–31
   Lykian funerary monuments 32, 36
   "Phrygian" tombs 41, 43n
   Thracian tholos tombs 39n160

ceramics
   and Hellenization 82–83, 85
   from Korinth 76
   in Karia 30
   in Sardis 18

Dorians. *See* Greeks

Ephesos 8, 14
   Cult of Artemis 16n, 17
Ethnic Identity. *See* Ethnicity
Ethnicity 2, 5, 6–7, 11, 55–56, 73
   emic vs. etic perspectives 68
Euromos 60

federations. *See* leagues

Gordion 8, 42n174, 43–44
   kingdom based at 41
Greeks 3–4, 53–54, 65, 67, 85
   Aiolians 7, 23
   Dorians 7, 75
   Ionians 2n2, 7, 13, 30, 53n, 81, 85n370, 87
gymnaseia 83–84

Halikarnassos 8, 28–29
Hekatomnids 25–26, 29, 70, 76–77, 82
   Maussolleion 30, 82
Helleno-centrism 2, 68, 73, 87
Herakleia Pontikê 8, 49, 63, 85
Hittites 64, 67
   imperial ethnography 1, 5, 48, 56–57
   relief sculpture 37
Hiyawa, kingdom of 51, 65–66
Hypaipa 17

Iasos 60
Ionians. *See* Greeks
Isaurians 3
Itlehi trmmili 33–35

Kabalians 7, 45–46
Kappadokians 7, 47–49, 64. *See also* Ariarathids
   rise of polis 77
Karkisa 57, 60–61
Kaska 57, 64
Katakekaumenê 8, 13–14
Kataonians 48
Kaunos 8, 24, 28, 60
Kibyra 8, 14–15, 46
Kilikians 7, 50–52, 65–66, 71, 75
   rise of *poleis* 77
   importation of Greek ceramics 82, 85
Koloë 8, 16, 17
Komana 9. *See also* Kataonians
Kybebe/Kybele. *See* Mother Goddess
Kytenion. *See* Xanthos

Labraunda 25, 30
Lagina 30
languages and names
   Karian 24, 28–29, 70–71
   Lydian 13–16, 58, 70

Lykian   33, 35–36, 71
Phrygian   43–44, 64, 71
Thracian   39, 64, 71
Laodikeia   8, 44, 87
leagues
　Chrysaorean   26–27, 75
　Kappadokian koinon   49
　Karian   25–27
　koinon of Galatians   40
　koinon of Greeks in Asia   74–76, 91
　koinon of Greeks in Bithynia   39
　koinon of Kilikians   52
　Lykian   35, 37, 45
Letoon   36–37
Limyra   8, 34–35
Lukka lands/people   48, 56–57, 62, 64
Luwians/Luwiya   58, 65
　hieroglyphic Luwian   21, 47, 50–51, 58
Lykaonia   8, 47, 64
Lysimachos   77

Macedonians   13, 18–19, 23, 43n182, 44, 85–86
Magnesia   7, 87
Mariandynians   7, 49–50, 63, 85
Masa   57–58, 64
Mermnad kings   12n, 13, 18–20, 22, 59–61
Meiones   12–13, 58–59
Men   53, 80–81
　Askaenos. *See* Antiocheia by Pisidia
Midas/Mita   40, 42, 44
Midas City   8, 43–44
Miletos   8, 29n101, 60–61
Milyans   7, 45
Mopsos   51, 65–66, 75–76
Mother Goddess   17, 43–44, 53, 80–81
　Lydian Mother   20
Mushku   42
Myceneans   56–57, 60, 65
Mylasa   8, 24, 28, 60, 74–75, 83

nationalism, influence of   53, 55, 66–67, 69, 77–78, 89
Nikaia   8, 39, 87
Nysa   27n94, 88

Oinoanda   8, 46, 82n356
Olbasa   46

onomastics. *See* languages and names
orientalism   90. *See also* nationalism

Pamphylians   7, 46–47, 65–66, 71n300, 75
Panamara   27n94
Paphlagonians   7, 49, 63, 72, 75
　royal foundations in region   88
Patara   8, 37
Pessinous   43n182, 44
Pergamon   8, 14, 23, 74
Persian Empire
　Iranians   18, 48–49, 67
　Iranianization   73, 78–79, 84
　satrapies   7, 18, 34, 43, 51, 61
　dahyava   10
Philadelphia   8, 13
Pisidians   45–46, 72, 75
　rise of *poleis*   77
　Pisidian gods   46
Pontos   9, 49, 57
　Pontic dynasty   48–49, 78–79, 84
　royal foundations   88
Ptolemaic Empire   26n89, 35, 51–52

Que. *See* Hiyawa

Religion
　acculturation   80–81
　in Kappadokia. *See* Kataonians
　in Karia   26, 29–30
　in Lydia   16–17
　in Lykia   36–37
　in Phrygia   44
Roman Empire
　influence on ethnic identity   20, 27, 35, 39, 40, 44, 46, 49, 74–75, 90–91
　Pompey   77
　Romans   3, 67
　Romanization   73, 79, 81, 82n357, 88

Sagalassos   8, 79, 85
Sardis   8, 12–14, 18–20, 59, 73–74, 76, 82, 90
　cult of Artemis at/near   16–17, 80–81
　cult of Zeus Polieus   17
　Lydian Zeus   20
Seleukid Empire   16, 19, 27, 51
Soloi   9, 66
Solymoi   37n152, 45

Sparta   12n, 75
Stratonikeia   8, 28, 86
Sura   48, 64

Tarsos   9, 66, 88
Telephos/Telepinu. *See* Attalids
Telmessos   8, 32
Termessos   8, 45, 71, 83n363
Thyateira   8, 13, 87
Tmolos, mount   8, 16
Torhebians   15–16

Xanthos (city)   8, 32–34, 75

Zeleia   43
Zeus
   Abretennos   24
   ancestor of Bithynos   38
   Chrysaoros. *See* leagues
   in Kilikia   80–81
   in Lydia. *See* Sardis
   in Lykia   36
   in Pergamon   22
   Karios   22, 24, 29
   Kretan-born   60, 74–75, 80–81
   Labraundos. *See* Labraunda
   Panamareus   29

Printed in the United States
by Baker & Taylor Publisher Services